How to Talk to Anyone About Anything

Improve Your Social Skills, Master Small Talk, Connect Effortlessly, and Make Real Friends

techniques outlined in this book.

By reading this document, the reader agrees that under no circumstances is the author responsible for any losses, direct or indirect, which are incurred as a result of the use of information contained within this document, including, but not limited to, — errors, omissions, or inaccuracies.

Table Of Contents

Your Free Gift

As a way of saying thanks for your purchase, I'm offering the book ***Bulletproof Confidence Checklist*** for FREE to my readers.

To get instant access just go to:

https://theartofmastery.com/confidence/

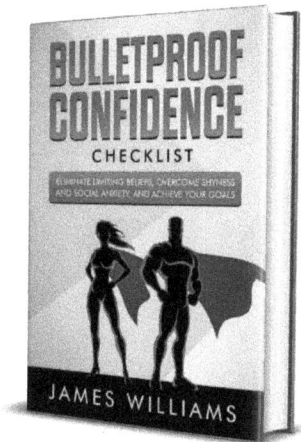

Inside the book, you will discover:

- Why we develop shyness & social anxiety
- Powerful strategies for overcoming social anxiety
- Become more confident by destroying these negative traits

- How to easily prevent the "awkward silence" in a conversation
- Confidence checklist to ensure you're on the right path of self-development

Introduction

Not too long ago, my friend Kyle came to me and told me a story of the weekend past when he had recently attended his sister's wedding. Kyle himself had been married for nearly twenty years before his divorce a few months prior, and this wedding was one of the first "outings" he attended by himself.

Over a beer, he told me about the big day. At ten, he was surrounded by friends and family, people he saw nearly every week, or at least sent a text message to every now and then. The ceremony was beautiful. Everyone was happy. They took taxis from the church to the reception held in this big fancy downtown hotel. Upon arriving, Kyle was busy making sure everything was running smoothly behind the scenes.

In true wedding fashion, people ate food, had some drinks, started dancing, and overall just let their hair down for a good time. Relatives from both sides of the new family came together to celebrate this wonderful occasion.

But for Kyle, it wasn't all smiles, booze, and confetti.

Plunged into the vast depths outside of his comfort zone, he told me that as soon as he started interacting with strangers, friends of friends, and distant relatives, he soon realized he had absolutely no idea how to talk to any of them.

He recalled a particularly embarrassing moment where his sister's new husband's cousin came over and said, "Hey," and he froze up, literally not saying a single word. Awkward was an understatement.

After the compulsory "How are you?" and "It's a beautiful service, right?" Kyle was stuck. His mind started to fill with anxiety. Endless thoughts bombarded him like, *What do I say? How can I make this person laugh? Do they even care about what I have to say? Who is this person? What are their interests?* and so on.

Outside his mind and back in reality, this all emerged as generic small talk, awkward silences, and uncertain looks towards the floor.

"God, it was terrible. Kathy (Kyle's ex-wife) was such a charismatic person, but I didn't realize how much she carried our conversations while we were married. I feel like I don't have the ability to talk to anyone. What do you talk about? Do people care about what I have to say? Even if they did, I don't think I have the confidence to even try. Lord knows how I'm ever going to start dating again, if ever."

As we finished our drinks and paid the tab, I told him that becoming confident, or even just speaking to other human beings, isn't some far-off idea reserved for only the most extroverted humans who ooze natural charisma. Oh no.

You see, over a decade ago, and then for most of my entire life, I was like Kyle. I went through school, college, university, and a scattering of first and part-time jobs and eventually on to the beginning of my career being awkward, shy, and withdrawn.

I was the guy who sat in the middle of the class, not cool enough for the back or smart enough for the front. I was the invisible one.

I had some friends I'd known all my life, but the older I became, the more social anxiety I felt, and the more isolated I found myself. It was crippling. I hadn't pushed myself to talk to anyone or had taken risks when meeting new people since I was a child. After all the passing years, it was like I'd forgotten how to do it at all.

It was hard to meet new people. I found it impossible to date. Speaking with the customers in my part-time jobs was messy, and selling to clients in my career was unreliable at best. I could only sometimes talk to someone without breaking a sweat or feeling like I was on the verge of having a panic attack. I had good days and bad days, but as years went by, I had two main realizations that ultimately led to me changing my life.

First, your connection to other people is everything.

Your relationships with others, your job, yourself, and your levels of overall happiness and life satisfaction are all determined by your ability to communicate and connect. You could have millions of dollars in the bank, have everything that someone can be deemed successful for having, but if you're lonely, you're not happy.

You can be poor and materially have nothing, but if you're surrounded by caring people with whom you share a meaningful connection, and you can feel like the wealthiest person on the planet.

My second realization was just as life-changing.

Being confident, charismatic, and open to connecting with others is *not* a trait you're born with. I used to believe that the confident people, those who could hold an entire audience or keep you hooked intimately on their every word, were gifted with a natural talent for confidence. I was wrong.

Confidence and charisma are skills that can be learned, honed, and practiced. They can even be mastered.

Have you ever gone into a room and saw that one person who dominates the conversation, maybe in a group of friends or in a meeting at work? Perhaps you had a friend who can seemingly speak to anyone about anything, and no matter the situation, they carry the flow of the conversation seemingly without effort? Ever found yourself envious of that person?

That's not the first time that person is doing that. You're seeing years of practice. Years of trial and error. Years of making mistakes, practicing new techniques, and learning from each experience along the way. They would have had awkward moments in school, embarrassing meetings, and conversations, where nothing seemed to work.

And this all raises more questions.

How can you do things differently? How do you become confident? How can you talk to anyone about anything?

I've been the shy guy. I spent most of my life as him. I was afraid of sharing my thoughts, and now I'm writing books you're reading (which still blows my mind to this day!). I can date people and hold my own. I can present meetings and engage everyone in the room. I can share stories with groups of friends and have them hang off my every word. I gave a talk in a public speaking group not too long ago, and a member of the audience came up and told me it was one of the best talks they had seen in years.

I'm not saying that to brag. I know my public speaking skills have a long way to go compared with the greats, but seeing my own journey of being the awkward kid to then being capable of speaking to a group of 30 people warmed my heart. If it's possible for me, it's possible for anybody.

Final questions.

How do you get better at swimming? You spend time in the pool.

How do you get better at writing? You write.

How do you get better at connecting with people? You connect with people.

Like all life skills, confidence is an act that's practiced and honed over time, but like an athlete needs a coach, I'm writing this book to help guide you along the path of your own journey. First, we're going to cover your mindset and get that in check, so you're actually ready for meeting new people.

Then we're going on to the real meat of this book. This is where I will cover subjects like how to start a conversation with someone, find similar interests, and guide the conversation with questions. You'll also find out how to be more charismatic and confident and how to act and present yourself in any situation you may find yourself in.

This book aims to be the key that will unlock so many doors in your life through connection and opportunities, so let's hang around no longer.

The Beginning

When it comes to making a change in your life, these are the three essential elements you're going to need to focus on:

Education. Awareness. Practice.

You need knowledge and information, so you know what decisions you're going to make. You need awareness to apply everything you've learned, to recognize where you go wrong, what you do right, and to be aware of where you need to get better.

Finally, you need to keep practicing and just keep getting better and better.

I've been on this journey.

During my mid-20s, I was unfulfilled and unsatisfied with my life. I lived in a big city with nobody around me that I could really call a close friend. No partner. It should have been an exciting time, starting my new career with high prospects, but I held myself back. I was ticking the boxes creatively, but I wasn't a people person, and people are the ones who give the opportunities.

I decided I needed to make a change.

I got educated. I read studies, scientific data, articles, and research reports. I read books and listened to podcasts. I took all this information and applied it in my own life, being aware of what I was doing so I could judge for myself what was right and what was wrong. I figured out what works for me, practiced it, and used these experiences to give myself the momentum to get where I am today.

The best thing about it all?

It works like an absolute treat.

Using my own experiences, scientific studies, and a ton of research, I've compiled this book to basically be everything you're going to need to know when learning how to speak with other people.

So, as we move into the true grit of this book, I want you to open your mind. Be willing to learn and take on board what you read. I highly recommend getting a pen and notebook to jot down ideas, techniques, and communication strategies that resonate with you, which will improve your ability to take them on board.

It's time.

Chapter One – Everything Starts with You

*"No matter who you are, no matter what you did, no matter where you've come from, you can always change, become a better version of yourself." – **Madonna***

When you first picked this book up, you probably read the title and created this image in your head of what it would actually be like to have the ability to speak with anyone. Maybe you have a fantasy of telling stories around the water cooler, everyone wide-eyed at how good your stories are.

Maybe it's the same with your dating life, and you crave to be the charismatic boy or girl that charms all who listen to you. Perhaps you want to communicate better with your colleagues, managers, bosses, or clients.

Yikes! I'm sure you're starting to see how vastly communicating with others literally affects every part of your life! However, I want you to put these fantasies aside for now (I promise we'll make them become a reality later) because we need to start with you.

Yup. It's time to take a long, hard look at ourselves in the mirror because guess what? There's a reason why people say, "You can't love other people properly until you learn to love yourself first." It sounds philosophical and perhaps something you've heard before, but hear me out.

We're going to make this actionable.

Let's start with the foundations of who you are, right here, right now. Your sense of self has to be defined because it will literally dictate how you act in every single situation from here on out, and you can either unconsciously let this happen, or you can be aware and in control of it. Don't worry; this will all make sense as we move forward.

A question to get the juices flowing:

Who are you?

Just consider and be aware of whatever thoughts come to mind. Now take those thoughts and drop the basic identity stuff, like your name, age, or your job. Now how do you see yourself? What kind of person do you associate yourself with? What beliefs and values do you have? Yup, we're jumping straight into the deep end here.

When I was 23 years old, and my self-development was beginning to take shape, I remember journaling one night for what must have been for one of the first times in my life (I had just watched a YouTube video on how *life-changing* it can be), and I asked myself these very questions.

Shockingly, I had no answers. What did I believe in? What did I value? Who was I? Well, I believe it's wrong to murder people. I believe that gravity exists. I believe that fast food should be eaten in moderation. As you can see, I was really scraping the barrel for ideas and didn't really have an answer with depth. I realized I didn't have a sense of self.

Your sense of self is everything. It defines you.

In the study of psychology, the sense of self is an all-encompassing view you have on yourself, your beliefs, your purpose in this world, and who you are. Guess what? If you don't know your own sense of self, how can you expect to *be* yourself when you're around others?

Having a sense of self motivates you to get up in the morning because you're fully aware of your mission in life and what causes you're fighting for. You know where you stand and what matters to you. Now, that's not to say your sense of self can't and won't change over time. In fact, if it didn't change, this can also be unhealthy, commonly known as being stuck in your ways. However, having some idea of your sense of self is vital. You cannot be confident without it.

Erika Myers, a professional counselor based in Oregon, sums it up perfectly.

"Having a well-developed sense of self is hugely beneficial in helping us make choices in life. From

something as small as favorite foods to larger concerns like personal values, knowing what comes from our own self versus what comes from others allows us to live authentically."

Authentic living. Isn't that the dream? No, it's not a dream. It's a **necessity**.

When you can learn to authentically be yourself *with* yourself, you can then begin to authentically be yourself with other people. You know how people say you can only really love others when you learn to love yourself? Well, we're playing on the same board as that ideology.

Being authentically you means you know you're not perfect (and that nobody is), but you're willing to accept your flaws and simultaneously embrace your strengths because they define you more than anything.

A lack of a sense of self is a problem.

Without any ideas of who you are or what you stand for, you'll find yourself drifting through life. You'll be uncertain and indecisive. Your life will lack momentum and drive. You'll feel anxious and unsatisfied, but you won't be able to put your finger on why because you don't understand what you want and don't want.

Remember my friend Kyle at his sister's wedding? In many ways, his whole sense of self had been derived from his marriage, and he didn't know who he was without it. When speaking with others at the wedding, he was drifting.

Was he there to have a good time? To simply show his face and support his sister? Was he there to meet new people? Was he looking to date someone new or even to hook up with someone? None of these things are good or bad because it depends on the individual and their wants or needs. However, without understanding what these wants or needs are, nothing can be done about them, and so the perpetual loop of anxiety continues.

Developing Your Sense of Self

To stress once again, you can't have relationships with others until you learn to have a relationship with yourself, which brings us nicely to your first exercise in this book. Don't worry. While it may sound a bit overwhelming, we're going to break it down and do this together. I got you.

Take a pen and paper and title it, *Checking in with Myself.* As it suggests, we're going to check in and explore who you are right now. Make sure you're in a quiet place where you can be with yourself and hear your own thoughts.

As defined by Healthline.com, your sense of self will fall somewhere on a spectrum. Either you have a solid, complete sense of self, none at all, or you fall somewhere in the middle. So let's figure out where you are.

Ask yourself some of these questions and write down whatever comes to mind. Also, I know what it's like reading books like this, and it's easy just to skim over these action points and try to do them in your head. If you want real change in your life (which is why I'm assuming you picked up this book in the first place), then actually take the time to do this activity, and see what happens.

If you're not proactive in actually doing something new, how can you expect anything to change? Anyway, that's something I wish someone had told me years ago. On to the questions!

> *What kind of person do you want to be?*
> *What kind of person are you right now?*
> *How would you describe yourself?*
> *Do you believe you've changed a lot over the years?*
> *What things in life are you good at?*
> *What things in life are you not so good at?*
> *What are you passionate about loving?*
> *What are you passionate about hating?*
> *What kinds of relationships do you have in your life?*
> *What kinds of relationships do you want in your life?*
> *How in control of your life do you feel?*

You don't need to answer all these questions, but if you look at one of them and think it's a bit difficult, then I recommend spending a bit *more* time answering it because that's where you'll find the interesting answers. Try to be as honest as possible.

Be aware that many of your answers will be influenced by how you see yourself as an individual and how others have told you they see you. For example, if your partner sees you as being lazy and always calls you that, you might start to believe you are actually lazy, even when you think, deep down, you're not. This is one of the ways you can acquire a *false* sense of self. This process is all about discovering your *true* sense of self, not just what other people and their views they've forced onto you.

The same applies in social groups, whether you're at school, in a friend group, with family, or in the workplace. You may act a certain way in order to fit in, but not actually be the person you're acting like. Try to cut through these false beliefs and write down who you actually think you are, for better or for worse.

When you're done, take some time to read back your answers.

Did you surprise yourself with what you wrote? Did things come up you hadn't thought about in a long time? Did you expect some of the answers? Did you tap briefly into a part of a "past you" you had forgotten about or thought was lost? Good. No matter what came up, clarity is on its way.

From here, take some time, maybe a couple of days or a week, to process what you wrote down. New ideas may come to you the more you think about this whole idea (so add them to your existing answers), and you may change your mind or have more certainty with other points you put down.

At the end of the week, read through everything once more, and move on to the next step.

Your Sense of Self is Born

With this information, like a phoenix from the ashes, it's time to be reborn as the true you.

This isn't something that will happen overnight, but a continuous process that evolves into a lifelong journey. As you have new experiences and learn new things, your sense of self will change and adapt, and that's a beautiful thing. What we're doing now is creating that initial foundation on which to build on.

I remember going through this process and being shocked by just how passive I was in my life. With family, friends, and coworkers, I adopted a different persona of trying to be who I thought these other people wanted me to be, rather than just being myself. I was living in anxiety, scared of judgment and rejections, and suppressing my true self the entire time. I craved freedom, and this is how I got it.

Set Your Values

Did you write down about how much you love animals or your passion for saving the planet? If so, it's time to start choosing cruelty-free brands and spending time getting more educated about the food you eat and the clothes you wear.

Did you write down how you value your health and looking after yourself? It's time to start working out and eating well.

Do you value relationships and experiences with others? It's time to call your mother and start organizing plans with friends.

Do you value genuine people and honest relationships? It's time to start thinking about what you're going to do about that toxic friend you've been trying to ignore.

Using the information you discovered about yourself in the previous section, you should be able to set at least some values that you believe in, all of which will then allow you to make choices in your life that you actually want to make. Life satisfaction and a sense of self will be derived from you making these choices.

What's more, you can learn to cut out the things that don't matter to you and don't serve your beliefs and values. I value connected relationships but felt lonely and didn't address my needs, so I plugged the gaps with video games.

Now, while I enjoyed computer games from time to time, I didn't enjoy playing them for six hours a day to stop myself feeling lonely, so I took action to only play for two hours on weekends and spent the regained time on my relationships. By making these proper choices, I naturally started to find balance in my life.

Set your values. Discover what matters to you. Make the right choices. Your sense of self will come from this action.

Having Proper You Time

The only way you can figure out what matters to you is by having proper quiet time with yourself, allowing yourself to listen to your thoughts and process how you're feeling. It's so easy to have a bad day and just numb it all out with TV, Netflix, and social media, but how are you going to learn about yourself if you don't think about it?

There are plenty of ways you can do this, whether you're a fan of reading or listening to music, or you can use some more hands-on self-help techniques, like journaling and meditation. It's entirely up to you, and if you're not sure, try a whole bunch of different approaches to see what works for you as an individual.

Get Help if Needed

The final point I want you to remember is that your self-help journey doesn't have to be one you go through alone. If someone you loved was going through this journey themselves, then it's pretty safe to say that if they needed help or support, you would help if you could. The same applies to you. People will always be willing to help you, especially if they're a loved one, but they need to know that you want the help first.

Suppose you're dealing with anything you can't seem to face, perhaps a mental health condition like depression or anxiety (both of which are very common with those who have a lack of a sense of self). In that case, professional guidance is always an option.

The Summary

And with that, we come to the end of the first chapter. Is the journey what you expected so far? Went a little deep, didn't we? It's okay. It's all essential, and what's amazing is that by focusing on just developing your sense of self, you'll instantly see real changes in your life and within your relationships with others.

Because you know yourself, you'll naturally be more confident in yourself. Since you know what you believe in, you can share your opinions with others and start to have more in-depth, meaningful conversations.

As a lightning-fast recap, you first need to focus on developing your sense of self by:

- Defining your values and beliefs
- Spending time getting to know yourself
- Understanding what makes you, you

As I said above, this is just the groundwork for becoming better at small talk, and if you want to go into this further, you're welcome to do some more research. However, in our journey together, we're going to pull back around to how to talk to anyone, starting off with one of the most essential skills you need to know.

Chapter Two – It All Begins with Listening

"When you talk, you are only repeating what you already know. But if you listen, you may learn something new." —
Dalai Lama

Chances are, you saw this coming. Every relationship you have, have had, and will have throughout your entire life is based and founded on effective communication. The most significant part of that is being able to listen to others communicating with you.

Listening is essential because you're giving someone attention that grants you clarity on what they're saying, and this is the best basis for a real relationship. Every human being wants to be heard and understood by others.

A 2015 study carried out by the Michigan State University backed this up and found that active listening (listening with intent) will enable you to talk more clearly and concisely with others and better understand the world.

Listening, therefore, not only improves your own speaking skills but also helps you connect with those around you. Imagine talking to someone who you can tell is not really listening to you. You've been there, right? It's horrible, and you don't want to be around that person for long. Let's explore how you can be a better listener.

The Two Types of Listening

Listening. You have a conversation, hear the other person, and respond to what they said, right? That's a conversation. Relationships are founded from this. Right? Simple stuff. Not entirely.

Research shows there are actually 18 different types of listening, including states of listening like biased listening, inactive listening, deep listening, empathetic listening, comprehensive listening, and so on. Still, for simplistic sake, I want to break it down into just two types.

> ➢ *Listening to understand*
> ➢ *Listening to respond*

When you speak to the vast majority of people, they will instinctively be listening to respond. This basically means that instead of *listening* to someone, this person already knows what point they want to share next, so they are, in essence, just waiting for the other person to finish speaking so they can have their turn.

A great example of this came up when I first dated my partner, and we went to visit her parents for the weekend. My partner had decided she would try a vegan diet after reading all the health benefits and didn't sit comfortably with the idea of eating an animal. Upon telling her dad, he replied,

"Why do you want to do that? Meat is so good. You know you'll never be able to eat burgers again?"

"Or delicious steak!" her mother chimed in.

My partner tried to explain, "Well, the impact of the meat industry on the rest of the planet is just not something I want on my conscience, and don't even get me started on how poorly the living creatures are treated."

To which he replied, "I couldn't do it. I just love steak too much."

Had my partner been listened to? No. As much as her dad is a nice guy, he has the thought process that meat is good and nothing can get in the way of that. It doesn't matter what my partner said; he would have stuck to his guns about how meat is amazing and the best thing ever.

They are listening to respond. To have a progressive conversation, he could have said something like, "Why? What are the health benefits? What impact does animal agriculture have on the planet?" and if he heard her out and still didn't mind eating meat, then at least he would have listened and given it a chance. They missed an opportunity to understand their daughter on an individual level simply by listening to her response.

The best, most meaningful conversations are based on everyone's aim within the conversation to understand each other, sharing what the facts are, and why people think and feel what they do. By taking this approach, you begin to understand others as individuals rather than force your own narrative.

How to Listen to Understand

This is logically the next question. So how do you listen to understand?

The same MSU study found, like most confidence and communication techniques, that listening to understand is a skill that can be learned and practiced, and to quote the report directly:

"Active listening takes time and practice. However, every time you use active listening, it gets a little easier. It can help you to navigate through difficult conversations. More than that, it helps improve overall communication, builds a better understanding, and ultimately leads to better relationships with family, friends, and coworkers."

Practice really does make perfect, so here are the skills on how to actionably listen to understand.

➢ *Give Your Full Attention*

This may sound obvious, but be honest with yourself; how many times are you listening to someone and you clock out, perhaps thinking about what you should be doing next, what's on TV later, or how you're going to respond? This isn't giving someone your full attention.

You can do this by:

- *Minimizing distractions, such as not playing with your phone or watching TV*

- *Make eye contact with someone*

- *Face the person you're speaking to*

- *Don't multi-task*

- *Bring yourself back to the present when you find yourself drifting*

A great trick I learned to help you keep focus is to concentrate on the center of your palm. You can do it now, and you'll notice how your attention travels there to the center of your hand. See how it makes your thinking stop and how much more focused you are? Try it in your conversations and see how effective it is.

I know this all sounds like simple stuff, but it's because it's so simple that it's easy to forget and get stuck in bad habits. A Harvard study as far back as 1957 even carried out courses to help people listen using these same techniques, which resulted in a 40% increase of people's listening capabilities, so try it for yourself!

➤ *Hear the Other Person Out*

When someone is talking to you, it's incredibly easy to fall into the habit of interrupting, which is a very bad habit. It also means you're not listening to understand the person, you're listening so you can now talk your own points, and that's not the foundation for a meaningful conversation. To help not interrupt people, you can:

- *Minimize distractions, so you're not answering a phone, for example*
- *You don't hold on to your point, but let it go and respond to what the other person is saying*
- *Wait until they have finished speaking*
- *Ask a question if you need more clarity on what they said, rather than just going back to your original point*

This is an important technique to think about because interrupting is a missed opportunity to understand the other person, but it also sends the message that you don't respect the other person enough or feel like their opinions are not worth listening to, and however you're interrupting them is more important than them.

This won't paint you in a favorable light.

➤ **Use Your Body to Listen**

Hand in hand with improving your listening skills, being conscious of your body and how you're controlling it can be a great way to improve how attentive you are. While I already mentioned making eye contact, you can do other things like:

- *Turning your body to face the person who's talking*

- *Nod occasionally*

- *Smiling, but not excessively (don't want them to think you're weird)*

- *Saying "uh-huh" to show you're engaged in the conversation and want them to keep going*

- *Adopt an open posture*

➤ **Repeat back their points for clarity**

One of the most popular ways to improve a conversation is always cited as being the repetition of a point. If someone says, "I like chocolate because it's sweet," you show you understand by starting your next sentence with "Because it's sweet? But which brand is your favorite?" Other ways you can do this include:

- *Paraphrasing what has been said by saying things like, "What I'm hearing is…" or "It sounds like you're saying…"*

- *Ask questions like "What do you mean by..." or "Do you mean..."*

- *Repeat key words back to the person every now and then*

That repetition of what the other person has said shows that you're taking on board and listening to what they have to say, meaning they'll feel like they can be a lot more open and connected with you.

> ➤ **Then Respond**

Since you've been actively listening to the other person, and they've finished speaking, now you can respond. You don't want to fall into the trap here of just going back to what you wanted to say originally, but instead, reply to what they're actually saying. You can do this by:

- *Addressing the key point of what they said, again for clarity*

- *Pause for several seconds that shows that you're thinking about what they said*

- *Convey your points in the best way possible*

Don't worry about this last section so much since the rest of the book is going to be dedicated to helping you know what to say in any situation, so we'll be covering this all in a lot more depth.

The Summary

By using these techniques alone, you'll notice such a huge difference in how connected you are to other people within your conversations and how you're being listened to yourself. When you listen to others and respect what they have to say, most people will unconsciously do the same back to you.

It's only when the other person doesn't feel listened to or respected that tempers start to rise, and things get out of hand. Remember, practice makes perfect, and even incorporating these points into your next conversation will make such an amazing difference. Try it for yourself!

For a quick reference, when listening to people, you're going to want to focus on:

- Understanding the two types of listening
- Practice listening to understand
- Avoid listening to respond
- Give someone your full attention
- Never interrupt someone
- Listen with your body, not just your ears
- Repeat back key points the other person said
- Respond to the point after everything else

And with that, we move on to the next chapter.

In one chapter's time, we're going to be focusing on the core mechanics of actually speaking to someone and starting a conversation, so if you want to skip ahead, that's no problem, but for clarity, the next chapter is going to explore some of the more advanced techniques you can use to actively listen more effectively.

Chapter Three – Further Listening Skills

"No one is as deaf as the man who will not listen." —
Proverb

A chapter that needs no introduction, since I did that a minute ago, so let's jump straight into it.

There are basically endless ways you can advance your listening skills, and since everyone is different, and we all have our own bad habits, some of these may apply to you, and some may not, but I like to think of this section as a great reminder of how to listen, as well as to help you set the overall intention of becoming a better listener.

Minimize Distractions

A study back in 2012 carried out by Larry D. Rosen Ph.D. researched 300 middle school, high school, and university students to see how distracted they became, depending on their environment. The students were supposed to be studying, although they were surrounded by phones, computers, and televisions.

The results were shocking, showing that when surrounded by technology, the students could only study for around **three minutes** at a time—laptops and phones providing the most distraction. Only three minutes. That's such a low attention span.

I understand life is busy, and things need to get done. Sometimes, multi-tasking is the only viable solution to make things happen since it feels as though there aren't enough hours in the day. However, if you want to have meaningful conversations and connect with people, there are going to need to be times when you sit down and talk to each other, without the distractions we're typically surrounded by. When someone is speaking to you, you can minimize distractions by:

- *Putting down and locking your phone*
- *Switching off the TV*
- *Turning off your computer monitor*
- *Not eating or drinking while talking with someone*

No matter where you are or what you're doing, whether you're at home or at work, these tips will make your conversations and your relationships far better.

Be Free from Judgments

It's crucial to think about how your judgments affect your ability to listen. If you're stuck in your ways and feeling rather close-minded or defensive on a subject, you can end up not actually listening to someone but instead zoning out or getting ready to tell them why they are wrong.

If you're able to step outside of that and open your mind, you may hear something and learn a new perspective. You may even sway your opinion or can give you more information to help solidify how you feel. Either way, you're going to grow as an individual by listening, so don't let the judgments stop you from doing just that!

To be less judgemental, focus on:

- Being more open-minded
- Notice judgments when they arise
- Become more accepting of other people's ideas
- Accept imperfections in people

Ask the Right Questions

Active listening to someone is all about understanding that other person, which is really all communication, in general, is about. Whether you're sharing thoughts or ideas or trying to solve a problem or even just entertaining, you need to be understanding, and people need to understand you.

Sometimes, people aren't going to be the best communicators, and you're going to require a little more information to understand them, and that's okay.

However, this is such an important element to think about that we're going to cover it in a lot more detail over the next chapter, so stay tuned!

The Summary

For now, these should be enough techniques and strategies to help you become the best listener possible. Some may seem basic to you, and some things you may never have thought of, so take your pick to see what you want to work on, and the chances are you should see positive results even with your first interactions from reading this chapter, so good luck, and see it all in action for yourself.

Let's continue our journey into the art of talking to anyone.

Chapter Four - It's All About Questions

"At the end of the day, the questions we ask of ourselves determine the type of people that we will become." — *Leo Babauta*

We ended the last chapter talking about the importance of asking the right questions, and it's a topic that deserves a lot of love. That's because when it comes to talking to anyone about anything, the best strategy you can ever have by your side is being able to ask the right questions at the right time.

It's pretty self-explanatory. Asking questions enables you to guide the conversation in whichever direction you want, helps you acquire clarity on what the other person is saying, and helps you find common ground and similar interests. Questions are everything!

Now, don't forget that you don't want to interrogate someone by bombarding them with questions. Instead, find a balance of asking questions and talking, just as it's important to get the topic of your questions right. When you bring together your newfound listening skills and mix them with your new ability to ask questions, you've got yourself a great conversation in the works!

The Power of Questions

You need to be direct with your questions and use this powerful conversational tool to make the other person feel like they can talk to you, to guide the conversation, and to make the other person feel understood.

We'll refer to each of these elements as:

- **Direction**
- **Clarity**
- **Understanding**

All of these are important when you want to engage in a proper, meaningful conversation.

Let's say you're talking to a colleague at work. It's Monday morning, and everyone is settling in for the day.

> *"Hey! How are you? How was your weekend?"*

> *"It was okay. Just watched Netflix, really. What about you?"*

> *"Yeah, it was good. Had a barbeque Saturday and just puttered about the house on Sunday."*

Not the most enthralling conversation of all time, but a pretty common one nonetheless. Now, you can use questions in a variety of ways here.

If you want direction, you could ask something like:

> *"What did you watch on Netflix? I'm looking for something action-packed myself. I just finished* Breaking Bad, *and I've got to say, it's pretty good."*

Now, through your questioning, you're guiding the conversation towards Netflix and TV series, which is a perfectly valid small-talk topic, especially if action-packed shows are something you share an interest in. You've taken control of the flow of conversation.

Other times, you're going to want some clarity, and this is useful for making sure you understood the other person correctly. You also make the other person feel like you really want to know more about what they have to say, thus making them feel more connected to you and more open with the topic at hand. Taking the same introduction as the last example, you get the reply:

> *"I got a new dog this weekend."*

How would you respond? Would you ask for its name? Its age? The breed? If you don't really know dog breeds very well yourself, then asking for the dog's breed isn't really a genuine question because as soon as they answer, you're going to be stumped with what to say next.

Never just go for the question you think is right, just because you're going through the motions. Really apply yourself to thinking of better, more progressive questions. This is what it means to ask the right questions.

Instead, what about asking something like:

"Oh yeah? How's he or she settling in?"

Interesting. Not a typical question. Requires a bit of thought. The person you're speaking with begins to engage more with the conversation.

"Yeah, not too bad, actually. He's starting to chew the edges of the sofa, though. He's quite young, so I don't know if he's teething or not."

What's your answer? Another question? What would you go for? It's really up to you. Just remember you've got three main options: Direction, Clarity, and Understanding.

If you want direction, you could say anything, depending on which aspect of the conversation you want to go into. Let's say you're not enjoying the dog conversation and want to move on. You could say something like:

"Might be a good excuse to get a new sofa. Or renovate completely. Would you if you could?"

You're redirecting the dog conversation to something a bit funnier or hypothetical. A bit lighthearted, if you will. If you instead wanted clarity—for example, you knew about dogs and their capability to bite through the corners of sofas—you might ask something like:

> *"Oh really? Is the dog chewing it all the time or just certain hours of the day?"*

Now you're seeking clarity and diving into the topic deeper. If, however, you want the other person to feel understood, you can repeat back what they are saying to make them feel heard.

> *"It could be an age thing if it's a puppy. Have you looked it up or spoken to a vet?"*

Of course, there are infinite ways you can guide the conversation based on the questions you ask, but this should give you a clear idea of how questions are so powerful when it comes to communicating and a massive part of talking to anyone.

Think of it this way. If you're asking questions and the other person is talking, you don't even need to be speaking most of the time, meaning there's little effort or chances to get anxious on your behalf!

Starting Conversations with Questions

Of course, one of the most powerful ways to use questions is by using them to *initiate* conversations in

41

the first place. However, you don't want to be boring. There's no denying the tried and tested questions like "How are you?" and "Where are you from?" are boring and too generic. These aren't the best ways to start a conversation. There are definitely better options to choose from.

So, let's break it down.

First, you need to get the conversation going. I'm going to assume you're not just talking to a random stranger on the street, but perhaps talking to a colleague at work, or a new client, as part of a networking event while on a date with someone, or so on.

As a side note, however, If you did want to talk to a stranger on the street, then always start with a conversation about something in the immediate environment, such as asking for directions, a good place to eat, the time, or commenting on something that is going on around you.

For example, if there's a carnival happening, you could ask something like, "When was the last time you went to one of these?"

For brevity, let's say you're talking to someone you know in a familiar place. It's time to get involved with some decent conversations. Here are some questions you could ask that can open a great conversation in various situations.

Meeting Someone New (Networking, social event, etc.)

Tell me something about yourself?

This is a great question because you let the other person take control and tell them what they want you to know, because of course, no one is going to tell you something they don't want you to know, allowing you to have a real insight into who this person is and what they're all about.

What was your highlight of this week?

This is one of my favorite questions because it allows the conversation to take a positive tone and allows the other person to really think about what matters to them. When they're thinking about positive things, they're going to be feeling positive emotions. It's far better than "How are you?"

Are you working on anything exciting at the moment?

Another chance for someone to get excited about talking to you, this question is ideal for when you want someone to be passionate with. Of course, they'll talk about the most important thing in their life, another great way to get to know someone and see what matters to them.

Have you been here before?

An open-ended question you can use to gauge someone's familiar with a place or person. If you're in a meeting or at an event, such as a business meeting, social event, birthday party (did you come last year?) and so on, you'll get a nice idea of how connected this person is.

Other questions you can ask when getting to know someone, especially on a professional level, include questions like:

- *Where did you go to school?*
- *What was your favorite part of school?*
- *How did you join this industry?*
- *Do you think your career path is similar to people like you?*
- *What's the biggest obstacle in your career?*
- *What's your favorite part of your job?*
- *Is your day quite varied?*
- *What does your typical workweek look like?*
- *What are your plans or aspirations for the future?*

- *What's it like working in your office?*

Of course, once you've asked these questions, these nicely lead to other questions you can ask that dive deeper into the topic you choose, depending on what answers they give you.

Questions to Ask While on a Date

- *What do you do in your free time?*
- *Are you a morning or night person?*
- *What would be your dream job?*
- *Who is the most interesting person you've met?*
- *How would your friends describe you?*
- *What song or artist do you never get tired of?*
- *What animal do you find the cutest?*
- *What animal do you find most ugly?*
- *What city would you love to live in?*
- *What is your greatest accomplishment?*
- *When was the last time you sang to yourself, and what song?*
- *What trends have you never been able to understand?*
- *What "thing" says the most about a person?*

- *What was the strangest turning point in your life?*

Fun, Personal Small-Talk Questions for Anywhere

Whether you're talking to your coworkers, friends, on a date, or just passing the time in a line somewhere, these are fun little questions you can ask anywhere.

There are a ton of fun questions you can ask people, and while they may sound a little out there, you'll usually find that people love answering them because they can have so many interesting answers, especially when you're with a group of people, allowing you to compare and casually critique each other's answers.

Basically, these are fun conversation starters that everyone can get involved in. Great for one-on-one or group chats!

- *What do you hope never changes in this world?*
- *What is your dream car?*
- *What's your guilty pleasure song?*
- *If you could learn any skill, what would it be?*
- *What do you wish you knew more about?*
- *How different was your life a year ago?*
- *What's the furthest you've been from home?*

- *If you could go to any fictional place, where would you go?*

Tips for Asking the Right Questions

Find the Line

Just a quick note, which acts as more of a disclaimer than anything else: Don't jump straight in and start asking really personal questions, or those on sensitive subjects, like race, sex, politics, religion, and so on. These can be hot topics, and while it would be nice to live in an ideal world where we can all talk about things openly without judgments, we're not quite there yet.

Instead, save these conversations for when there's a right time and place to speak about them, or you're with people you trust and are comfortable enough with to have these conversations.

Remember Social Hierarchy

Personally, I think it kind of sucks that we can't just be ourselves around everyone (and I know, a lot of what I've said already is about being yourself), but for many other people, you won't be able to connect with them unless you speak to them in a way they're going to understand.

For example, if you're talking to a peer or colleague, you're going to use different language and come across differently than if you were talking to your boss. Similarly, you would talk to the president or the Queen of England differently.

When speaking to others, try to adapt the way you talk and the questions you ask in a way that will be most effective to the listener. If you're talking to a client and they're quite a fancy person, then talking in a genuinely "fancy" way is going to make them connect with you far more than if you fill your sentences with slang.

>*"Ah, yes, we're very excited about the project here. What are your thoughts on it so far?"*

>*"Yeah, the project's lookin' good. You excited to get going?"*

The question is the same in both instances; it's just how it's framed that makes all the difference.

Keep Your Questions Open-Ended

Finally, always try to keep your questions as open-ended as possible because you're inviting someone to give you a comprehensive answer.

>*"How are you?"*

>*"Good."*

That is not a great conversation.

"What was the highlight of your week?"

"Nice question. Let me think. Probably getting a panini for free in my favorite cafe because they know me and were being nice."

"Wow, that's cool they did that. How long have you been going there?"

Far more interesting. While on this note, you can make questions more open-ended by changing them to include words like what, who, and how. You can also say, "Tell me more," allowing someone the opportunity to elaborate on what they're saying.

With that, you should now understand how important it is to ask questions in your conversations and the benefits you can enjoy by doing so.

The Summary

Just to recap this chapter, you're going to want to remember to:

- Ask lots of questions to get to know someone
- Keep the questions open-ended using words like what and how
- Use questions for conversational direction, clarity, or for further understanding
- Have a backlog of go-to questions to remember depending on the situation

- Don't get too personal or head into sensitive subjects

Armed with this new information, I'm now going to take you down a different rabbit hole, and that's being able to talk to someone in the first place, no matter what situation you're in.

Chapter Five - How to Have a Conversation with Anyone

"Good conversation can leave you more exhilarated than alcohol; more refreshed than the theater or a concert. It can bring you entertainment and pleasure; it can help you get ahead, solve problems, spark the imagination of others. It can increase your knowledge and education. It can erase misunderstandings, and bring you closer to those you love."

— Dorothy Sarnoff

This next chapter is pretty much the crux of this book.

Within the next few pages, I'm going to share with you and explore a literal step-by-step way you can have a conversation with anybody about anything. We'll talk more about what you can talk about and how to carry these conversations to be even better in the following chapters, but for now, we're going to cover the absolute fundamentals, building the foundations for your next conversations to stand on.

Ready? Let's go.

Step One - First Impressions

First impressions always count, so how do you want yours to be perceived in the eyes of others?

After all, you have complete control over it, even if it may not seem like it at times.

As a quick note, this section could also cover topics like dressing well, dressing for the occasion, making sure your personal hygiene is up to scratch, and so forth because these are all very important points to remember if you're looking to connect with someone and make a positive first impression.

However, sticking with the interpersonal conversational skills side of things, whenever you meet someone new, you're going to want to create a first impression that helps them connect with you. After all, while we're taught to never judge a book by its cover, let's be honest: We all do this all the time. If you head into a meeting with a new client or go on a first date, you judge that person to see if they're someone you want to work with or spend more time with.

Moreover, while you're giving your first impression to them, they also give one to you. So what does theirs say? Lots to think about, but let's cover both sides of this first impressions coin.

Reading the Room

Remember when you were in school, and your teacher would call in sick, and you'd have a substitute teacher in to cover for them?

I remember having one in my French class, and for the first few lessons, everybody would behave and stay reasonably quiet. While this was quite unconscious, it's clear in hindsight that we were trying to suss out whether the teacher was incredibly strict or a bit of a pushover. As we became more comfortable and pushed the limits, we started to misbehave, which most children do, more and more.

As soon as it was clear the teacher was trying to be a "cool" teacher and wasn't going to crack a whip in our direction for the slightest problem, the class slowly began a descent into chaos.

This same logic applies in your own conversations and interactions.

Whenever you go into a new interaction, start by reading the other person and seeing what type of person they are. Test the waters and see what kind of feedback you're getting. Some questions to ask and things to focus on include:

- *What kind of tone of voice are they using?*
- *What clothes are they wearing?*
- *Are they busy?*
- *Are they at work or relaxing?*
- *Do they look stressed out?*
- *Are they smiling?*
- *How firm is their handshake?*

- *How on time to meet you are they?*

- *What is their body language telling you?*

- *How polite are they?*

- *What manners do they have?*

- *What does your gut instinct say about them?*

Some people are a lot easier to read than others, and you may instantly know the kind of person you're talking to, especially if they're very forthcoming. Alternatively, you may need to gauge a little and start the conversation flowing to really get a feel for who this person is, and therefore, how you're going to effectively communicate with them.

For example, if someone is withdrawn, are they shy, or are they trying to hide something?

The situation you're in will provide a lot of context. The trick here is to look past what the person is saying and instead read their body language and all the other factors we just spoke about. However, someone's body language is very important.

Research shows that around 55% of all communication happens through body language, and 30% happens through tone of voice, so be conscious of it!

Some tricks to remember when reading body language include;

- *Posture. Is someone's head up and confident, or unsure and looking at the ground, avoiding eye contact?*

- *Appearance. What clothes are they wearing? Casual? Smart? Relaxed? Doesn't care?*

- *Crossed arms and legs tend to portray defensive feelings*

- *Hands in pockets (or hidden hands) suggest the person is hiding something*

- *Lip biting or nail picking can be a sign of feeling under pressure*

- *Facial expressions*

By observing these traits, you should be able to read the other person you're speaking with quite well, and then you can use this information to respond in the way that seems appropriate. Remember, people will respond to you how they perceive you are speaking to them, so adapt how you talk for the best results. Once you start getting to know somcone and go deeper with them, you can start showing more of yourself.

An example of this initial conversation may be speaking to someone who is looking shy, stressed, or sad. If you read these kinds of signals, you may want to approach them in a nicer, more compassionate way than you would normally speak to someone.

Even if you're finding it hard to read someone, remember: Your gut instinct is usually right when it picks up on cues, so trust it.

Research shows that people who are more tuned into sensing their body sensations in high-pressure situations (in the case of the study, they were looking at people who worked in high-stress London trading floors) were making better, more successful decisions than those who were out of sync with their gut instinct.

In other words, if you have a feeling and your body makes you feel a certain way, it's trying to tell you something, so let it guide you!

Writing the Room

Hand in hand with the point above, it's important to use the information you've learned to take control of your own first impressions and adjust how people are perceiving you. If you walk abruptly into a room and you're crashing around and stumble and then hide in the corner, this creates a very different impression to one who walks in and sits down gracefully and with confidence.

You have control of this!

Some quick-fire points to think about include:

- *How you are dressed*
- *Your tone of voice when speaking*
- *What does your body language say about you?*
- *The firmness of your handshake*
- *Are you making eye contact with the other person?*
- *Are you staring too much?*
- *Are you giving someone your full attention, or are you distracted?*

Be mindful of how you're portraying yourself in the eyes of others, and you'll get a reaction based on what you do. This gives you full control of a situation when talking to anyone, which is going to make you feel far more confident in your abilities to talk to someone.

Another great example of this comes from Patrick King's *Better Small Talk.* In his book, he talks about children and how they haven't developed the social filters many of us develop as we grow older. We have insecurities, anxieties, and traits that children don't yet possess. This is why when we talk to children, we talk to them in a certain way based on how they are talking to us.

In most cases, younger children will just act like themselves. This is why kids happily cry in public or act the same in front of elderly relatives as they do with younger family members. Kids are themselves, usually to funny or embarrassing ends.

However, the confidence that children have with just being themselves means that they are confidently writing the room around them, in which adults will follow suit and will respond a certain way. This is why it's so easy to talk to children, because they can speak with such confidence, without censorship, while being so forthcoming.

Step 2 - Making the First Move

There's no denying that so many of us put so much pressure on "breaking the ice" and making the first move, almost certainly to the extent that so many of us are so afraid to speak first that we end up not speaking at all. Over time, we've ended up where we are now and having to retrain ourselves to be more confident. There's such a huge fear that we'll be rejected by the other person, judged, or hurt in some way, even if it's just asking a stranger on the street for directions.

Really let that sink in and realize how true that is for many people! However, making the first move is essential if you want success in your conversation, and that's not just success in making them happen in the first place. A study found that making the first move results in so much success in so many areas of your life. In business, making the first offer puts you more in control and more likely to get a better deal. In dating, making the first move is more likely for you to get what you want.

But how do you build the confidence to do it?

The reality of the situation is that breaking the ice and making the first move isn't really that hard. All you need to do is "cut the fluff" and go straight for what you want. I could say just be confident, don't put too much pressure on yourself and the end result, but instead, be in the moment, but I'm guessing that doesn't really help, so let's break it down.

Take dating as an example (I like using this example a lot, but that's because we tend to add so much pressure to ourselves in these situations, most of the time so unnecessarily).

There's a whole taboo subject that you need to have "game" when trying to ask someone out. You need to be slick and have "tactics" to make it work, but this isn't real life, and it's not going to get you to where you want to be.

For some reason, we've forgotten that just going up to someone and being our genuine, authentic selves is easily the best way to get someone's attention and will develop a much stronger connection over the long term. This, of course, applies to all situations, not just dating.

Still, that doesn't help you make the first move. You may feel like you're inconveniencing someone by talking to them, holding them up, or interrupting them. You may not want to speak to a stranger in case you disturb them or they find you annoying. This is social anxiety in full swing.

The actionable step here?

Indirectly approach someone for something, for some reason, and have this reason clear in your head at all times, but don't make it a long-term reason. Don't think, *Wow, I want to talk to this person because I want to date them and marry them* and so on.

Thinking this way means you're putting far too much pressure on yourself because if you're rejected, it's going to hurt. There's too much focus on the outcome, and it's going to make you buckle when the conversations feel too much.

Start small. Think, *Hey, this person seems nice. I'll ask if they want to FaceTime or go for dinner*. Asking someone to go to dinner is way smaller a commitment than thinking long term, and you don't even need to have the pressure of this kind of event if it's too much.

Create a reason to speak to someone, even if there isn't one. Again, this is a fantastic thing to practice because it gives you the chance to try something new, boost your confidence, and get better at speaking with people. Most interactions will not be the most important ones you'll ever have, so relax and try to have fun with them!

Some of the things you can say or ask include:

- *Do you have the time?*
- *Where is the closest bank?*
- *Is the food good here?*
- *What time is the show starting?*
- *Have you seen this movie before?*
- *I love the music here. Do you?*
- *Do you know anyone here?*

These are all small statements you can ask to break the ice, opening the doorways for engaging small talk and conversation, and ultimately deeper connection, should you want to continue speaking with them.

Step Three - Find the Connection

Now you're talking with someone you've approached the right way, the ice has broken, and the conversation is starting to pick up and find its pace. What do you do now?

The best approach for finding a connection is to find similarities you have with that other person. This means finding common ground on things you're interested in, whether that's a hobby, passion, or music taste, or even just commenting and sharing opinions of what is happening in the immediate environment or situation you're in. An example of the latter would be commenting on the music at a concert you're at.

This is where your listening skills come into play because you're focusing on what someone is saying (and what their body language is saying) and then picking out the bits they seem most connected to, then running with it. Let me give you an example.

Let's say you're at a concert and you're engaging in small talk with someone at the bar. Your first impression is that they are not really having a good time. They just look into their drink, not really focusing on the music, and seem to be mentally somewhere else.

Everything about them suggests they're having a rough time, so you choose to act compassionately and ask if everything's okay, perhaps saying something like, "Is the music too loud for you?" This is lighthearted, not too personal, but also suggesting that you know that something isn't right, and you're willing to talk to them about it.

Depending on their answer, you can then figure out what's wrong and how you can deal with the situation, and you could be on the road to making a close friend.

In any given situation, depending on the context, you can find things in common by asking things like:

- *Where did you go to school?*
- *Where do you work?*
- *What sports team do you support?*
- *What music do you like?*
- *What food is your favorite?*
- *Where do you like to eat?*
- *What kind of movies do you like?*

It's also important to make sure you're vocal about what you agree on. It's all well and good thinking ("Hey, me too!"), but you're not going to connect with the other person unless you tell them that you're on the same page. Vocalizing this is a great way to build rapport and to make someone want to connect with you, which leads us nicely to the next point.

The Mastery of Mirroring

Mirroring is such an important part of any conversation because it makes you more relatable to the person you're speaking to. Mirroring is basically a practice where you're consciously copying (but not too obviously) the tone of voice, posture, body language, speed of speech, and overall physical appearance of the person you're speaking to, which dramatically improves how connected people feel to you.

You can also mirror based on the language and visual style that someone is speaking to you in, such as the amount of slang they're using, but sticking with physical mirroring is enough for most conversations.

A study (Anderson, 1998) also found that people felt more positive towards strangers when mirroring occurs.

Taking the bar example above, if someone is leaning at the bar slouched, and you pull up next to them and do the same, this is mirroring. If they speak slowly and without enthusiasm, mirroring this will help them take on board what you're saying more effectively because you've already created common ground through physical acts alone.

Some things to remember to mirror someone properly include:

- *Mimicking voice speed and tone*
- *Copying volume of gestures*
- *Copying body language, such as posture and leaning*
- *The inflection on certain words*
- *Usage of slang*

- *The energy and excitement for a topic*

You know when you meet someone, and you discover that you share a love for the same band, movie franchise, or sports team, and there's that moment when you look at each other like, "Oh my god, you love them too? That's amazing!" and your energy levels spike, and it's like you both build momentum with each other? That's the magic of mirroring in full effect.

Step Four - Addressing Obstacles You May Face

If you follow the three steps above, you'll be able to converse with anyone about anything, so that's where we'll end the book. Thanks for reading. Enjoy your day.

I'm joking, of course. In an ideal situation, you'll follow these points, and people will respond to you positively, and the conversations will be able to flow naturally from here on out. However, not everybody is relatable in such a way, and talking to some people can be less enthralling than chatting with a brick wall.

This can happen for many reasons: whether the person is having a bad day, is surprised by you talking to them in the first place, is stressed out, is shy and anxious, or just isn't in the mood for talking. When you talk to people like this, and the conversation feels like it's scraping by with friction, it can be hard to know what to do next. Do you force the conversation to go further, or do you cut and run?

First, remember you can always leave a conversation if you don't want to continue. Just say something along the lines of "Oh, I've got to dash to make the train/get some food/meet someone else," and so on, and you can just leave.

However, there may be times when you need to talk to someone, such as conversing with someone at work, trying to get a job done, interviewing someone, networking, or trying to get information from them. Don't worry; that's not as malicious as it sounds. Imagine you're trying to organize a surprise party for someone and need to know their schedule without actually telling them what's going on. How can you press the conversation forward?

Perhaps the most common technique to use here is elicitation, a communication technique developed by the FBI for interrogation purposes. Now, I'm not advocating that you go out and interrogate people for information—far from it. Teachers use this technique in the classroom all the time, although perhaps without realizing its origins.

Elicitation is the process of getting people to share information that they are holding on to by using statements that guide the person into speaking, even if they don't really want to.

An example of this would be to recognize and compliment someone. Human beings, while complex, are really rather simple when it comes to how we work. We are social creatures who are instinctively wired to receive praise and recognition from others because it shows we're being accepted into a larger group, which back in the day would have been essential for our survival in tribes and larger groups.

Giving someone a compliment about how they are or their physical appearance can be a great way to get them talking. Some statements you can use include:

- *I really like your coat. It suits you.*
- *Damn, I love how hardworking you are.*
- *Your attention to detail is incredible.*
- *The way you express yourself is great.*

Another way to engage in elicitation is to complain, and as I'm sure you know, human beings love to mutually dislike someone, whether it's an opposing sports team, the grey weather, or just a mutually shared situation, like having to stay late after work to get a project completed.

People love to complain. Studies even show that the average person complains between 15–30 times a day, and ActofLibraries.com rates "starting a conversation" as their number one reason for complaining in the first place.

A quick complaint into something can be a very powerful way to open people up and get them speaking, especially if they're looking to vent about a situation they're dealing with.

With all this in mind, next time you watch a crime thriller or detective series when a police interview is taking place, you may start to notice these tactics in full effect. I recently sat down to watch *Breaking Bad* again and (mild spoiler alert) saw the episode where Brock is poisoned, and Jesse has to go into the police station to say why he believes Brock was poisoned by a super-rare substance.

The detectives say things like:

- *We don't need to get the lawyers involved. It's all pen-pushing and a lot of hassle.*

- *We know these situations can be stressful. Just relax. We're just chatting.*

- *You're a smart guy, Jesse.*

- *You're a kind, caring guy. We know you only want to do what's right.*

Even in a situation like where someone is being interrogated for a supposed crime, the detectives use compliments to encourage them to talk, even if they don't want to.

And with that, we come to the end of this chapter. As an actionable recap, when it comes to starting a conversation, you'll want to:

- **Read the other person**
- **Aim to create the first impression you want to give**
- **Break the ice with a question**
- **Have a goal in mind for the conversation**
- **Find similar interests**
- **Find the connection you share**
- **Mirror the person you're speaking to**
- **Practice talking to unresponsive people**

Chapter Six – Mastering the Art of Small Talk

"Small talk is the biggest talk we do." — **Susan RoAne**

The main problem my friend Kyle had while attending his sister's wedding was not being able to get the conversation off the ground in the first place, and I know from personal experience that that's one of the hardest parts of meeting and getting to know new people.

A few years ago, I spent a lot of time on dating apps like Tinder and Bumble before I met my current partner, and I always struggled with what the hell I was going to say after the initial "hey" (which was usually followed by a cringey waving emoji, but I won't go further into that). But then again, what are you supposed to say to be interesting, charismatic, and genuinely be someone that someone else wants to speak to?

Throughout other times in my life, like lining up at the gym to go into a spinning class, I'm surrounded by strangers, and you say the generic small talk stuff about the weather and the problems and politics of the gym, poor management, and so on, but where do you go from there? You're not exactly going to make best friends with someone with that kind of talk.

That's what I'm dedicating this chapter to—mastering small talk.

Every single relationship you've ever had (except that with your parents, maybe your siblings) would have started with small talk of some kind. A test of the water to see whether the person is someone you connect with or not, someone you want to be friends with or not, a client or business is one you want to work with or not, and so on.

Mastering this art, like listening, will take a bit of practice, but with the knowledge we're going to explore in this chapter, you'll have everything you need for success. So, let's get into it.

The Core Strategies of Small Talk

To start with, it's worth noting that much like listening, the art of small talk has seemingly infinite depth, and it's a lifelong skill you can always work on improving. With over nine billion people on the planet, there's always going to be a new way to get through to someone and a new way of talking to learn.

That being said, we can actually boil the art of small talk down to just four core foundations that everything else is built on. Fortunately, the first three steps are points you already know: to ask questions (especially open-ended ones), be proactive with your listening, and minimize distractions.

So, what's the fourth, mysterious foundation? Any guesses?

It is, in fact, showing enthusiasm. Bringing energy into your conversations. Showing you're passionate. Resonating vibrancy into your interactions. You can talk about anything, and it can be engaging as long as you have enthusiasm.

The Power of Enthusiasm

Small talk may not be the most interesting thing in the world, but that's only the generic small talk we've all become so painfully used to. Showing energy and enthusiasm for connection can be such a powerful gateway into having a deeper relationship, no matter what you're talking about, and helps the person you're speaking with open up and be themselves, thus nurturing a meaningful relationship even further.

Even if you just act enthusiastic about even the most mundane conversations, you'll see a turnaround in how you connect with people. Try it now in your head. Imagine a standard conversation with someone in your life, and now imagine that same conversation with three times the enthusiasm and imagine how they'd react. I'm not saying you need to be like this all the time, nor do you need to give it ten times the energy when you're talking about traffic. You pick your times and places to go all in.

Adding this degree of energy to your conversations is all about your attitude and your intentions. When you go into any conversation, professional or personal, friends or family, lovers or children, if you have the mindset that you want to know more about this person, or you just want to have fun or learn something new, suddenly you'll start viewing human interaction in a completely different way, and subsequently, life changes.

You'll soon realize that there are endless people out there to meet, infinite views and perspectives to learn from, and fun stories and experiences to share, and isn't it these kinds of values that you wanted when you picked up this book in the first place?

So, how do you do it?

It can be hard to bring enthusiasm to a conversation, especially if you're not a particularly energetic person by nature, and going above and beyond how you would usually be may make you feel fake or as though you're not really being yourself, but this isn't a direction you want to head down. You want your energy levels to be genuine.

Fortunately, there are plenty of ways you can do this.

> ### *Act More Energetic*

Even adjusting tiny details in the way you converse can make such a big difference. You can talk a little louder in terms of volume (I'm not saying shout, but you know what I mean), and you can change your tone of voice to make it more diverse. You can also emphasize certain words and adjust your inflection to make what you're saying more interesting to listen to.

For example, take the two sentences below:

> *I got a new cat over the weekend.*

> *Oh my, I got my NEW cat over the weekend, and she's so CUTE!*

The emphasis is on the large words, and you can see how just slightly adjusting what you're saying can bring so much more power to your words.

You can, of course, amplify your body language to enhance what you're saying as well. For example, instead of saying, "Well, you have two choices. A or B?" you can use your hands to highlight the options, indicating them right for A and left for B. You're not really pointing at anything, but you're amplifying the fact there's a choice to be made and two options to choose from.

Overall, this kind of action makes the conversation seem more interactive.

➢ *Highlight How You Feel*

You don't need to agree with everything everyone ever says to you for them to like you. In fact, it's better if you surround yourself with people of opposing views because it helps you stop being stuck in your own ways.

There will be things you disagree with, just like they'll be statements that resonate with you, but whichever you feel, highlight that this is how you're feeling. This is one of the best ways to bring energy into a conversation because it's a great way to simply be yourself.

For example, if someone says something you resonate with or says something that you couldn't have said better yourself, then tell that person that that's how you feel. Check out these statements:

Yes! I completely agree. You worded that way better than I ever could!

I'm so glad you brought that up. I feel the same!

Wait, you're interested in that too?

I see what you're saying, but I'm the opposite. I love XYZ.

I really don't agree with you. I really feel like...

See how much energy statements like these can bring to a conversation and how validating it will feel for the other person?

Be genuine and say how you feel. When you're being open and honest, the conversation becomes less placid and passive and is instead more direct and assertive.

> ### *Exert Natural Energy*

A really quick note here. I'm not here to tell you how to live your life on a healthy level, but it's common knowledge that if you look after your body, you naturally have a ton of untapped energy that will naturally rise up in the way you live your life.

By this, I mean exercising regularly, eating well, drinking lots of water, getting enough sleep each night, and so on. If you look after yourself, you'll naturally have more energy. This may all sound a little basic, but hey, I know for a fact that I used to not really look after myself properly, and taking control of that bought about a lot of positive changes.

> ### *Surround Yourself with the Right People*

Granted, you're not going to be around positive, happy people at every waking moment of your life, nor would that be a healthy thing. Sounds like some weird cult thing happening in that world. However, you do need some stable positive people in your life that you spend regular time with if you want to adopt these personality traits yourself.

Negativity is physically and mentally draining, and you're not going to feel energetic or on the ball in any sense if you feel depressed and drained. It just won't happen unless you're incredibly passionate about faking how you feel.

Seek out to spend time with people who fill you up with energy, make you feel good, and consistently don't bring toxicity and negativity into your life.

Discovering Engaging Small-Talk Topics

Okay, so you're following the tips above, and you're starting to bring your own brand of energy into your conversations.

It doesn't matter where you are or who you're speaking with—you're attractive to listen to. You're also listening to the other person, you're asking questions, and everything seems to be running smoothly. I'm sure you're able to see how everything we're spoken about already is coming together to ensure your conversations are perhaps like no other conversations you've had before.

Notice how at the beginning, I said being charismatic and confident is something that can be learned? Take a moment to think about everything you've learned so far and how applying this information will evolve your relationships and interactions. Perhaps you've already tried it yourself, and you're starting to experience the results? Fortunately, there's more to discover.

A question we've already run into time and time again is what actual topics you can talk about. While there are practically infinite topics to talk about, it can be hard to remember the best ones, and while someone may care a lot about one topic, another person could have no interest whatsoever, leaving you stuck with no ideas on how to move forward. This section is here to help.

Jumping straight into it, here are some great topics to have in your back pocket that you can pull out in any conversation.

- ➢ Talking about the location you're in (immediate environment)
- ➢ Food, restaurants, and cooking
- ➢ Travel, vacations, holidays, dream destinations
- ➢ Sports
- ➢ Hobbies and passions
- ➢ Art
- ➢ Favorite local places

When you head into a conversation with someone, if you're listening carefully (which is why we covered this skill in the first chapters), you can pick up clues that can help you identify which topics are best to engage in. Here's an example conversation of two people waiting quietly at a bus stop on a grey rainy day.

A: Hey. You okay? You're looking a bit down.

B: Yeah, I'm fine. I've never much been a fan of waiting or the rain.

See how they start talking about the weather? It's a typical small talk conversation commenting on the immediate environment, which makes it easy to talk about, but what's interesting is the fact person B used it as an excuse for not feeling okay right now. All this is picked up on by listening to one sentence.

A: Oh yeah, more of a sun worshipper?

B: Yup. Any day of the week.

A: Where would you go if the bus could take you anywhere in the world?

A beautiful transition away from traditional small talk and into a more interesting topic of conversation that's open-ended enough for them to answer however they want. If they reply creatively, you know the person is down for actually talking. If they're pretty blunt and answer with something like, "Hm, I don't know," then you know they're probably not in the mood.

> B: *Probably south of France. I love it down there. The sun is beautiful on the coast.*

> A: *Oh, right. Have you been before? I'd love to go there myself.*

And so on.

More than you probably realize, people will give you topics to talk about in everything they say because they're already thinking about themselves and how they perceive the world at all times. In this example, Person B loves going abroad and being in the sun, and this is a fact that shines through in the very first thing they say.

Notice how person A ends with "I'd love to go there myself," bringing that energy and passion into the conversation that invites person B to open up more and start sharing the energy they have for something they love—in this case, warm countries. They don't seem very engaged in the conversation at first, but they can start to be themselves in just a few sentences. The conversation begins to find a rhythm.

You Will Need to Carry the Conversation... At First

You may feel this kind of conversation feels very one-sided, with you doing all the talking and the other person not really asking you questions but unfortunately, that's just the way things are these days for many people. That's not to say that everyone is like that, but there are multiple reasons why.

Either people love talking about themselves or, especially if they're talking with a stranger, won't think to ask them about their life, or are too afraid to ask because they feel like they're being intrusive. Other people may not be used to talking to other people so openly, so it can take a little while for them to open up and come out of their shells.

There are endless reasons how we've reached this point. Studies and research suggest that we're drifting apart from each other, or we're so reliant on social media that we're losing our social communication skills. There are many studies out there, like the 2018 study on "Social Media Use and Perceived Social Isolation Among Young Adults in the U.S," that social media use is a massive contributing factor to ever-growing feelings of isolation and loneliness, suggesting that we're disconnecting from one another in a way like never before.

However, everyone is different, and whatever the reason for someone being too withdrawn to talk to you and step out of their own shell, you have the tools to help the people you speak with to come out of the other side and realize we don't have to be so closed off with each other.

Meaningful Relationships Take Time

Going back to my line in the gym for a spinning class example, there are plenty of things to talk about with others around me. I could talk about the quality of the class, the music choice, how easy it was to park outside this evening, gym announcements that have been made, and so on.

These might not initially sound like interesting subjects at first, but that doesn't make them any less essential. Remember, you should try not to be judgmental since you never know what you're going to learn or what topics of conversation will arise as a result of the typical small-talk topics.

What's more, having small talk with easy topics first is essential for opening the door to deeper conversations down the line. If you're talking to someone, you need to build up your connection with them to lead to deeper, more meaningful subjects.

Trust and respect are key parts of any relationship, and they take time to build up.

A really beautiful example that illustrates this point comes from my mother and father trying pottery classes when they first retired. When catching up, they would tell me about the boring conversations they had at first, and perhaps these classes weren't for them. It was all small talk and no substance, gossip, and the sorts, which didn't really interest my parents. I told them to hang in there and give it time. It was only like this because they were new, and the relationships were forming.

Over time, they came to know that one of the other attendees, Maisie, was going through a battle with cancer, and while on a Sunday afternoon walk, they took flowers and chocolates to her house as a surprise and had an afternoon of tea. Their relationship kept going, and once Maisie had recovered from her therapy, my parents, Maisie, her husband, and a few others from the pottery class even went on vacation together.

All these opportunities started with small talk in a pottery class on those first few sessions. Every relationship needs to start somewhere.

This is why it's a good idea to have some key go-to small-talk topics up your sleeve that you can pull out at any time. I know we've covered a lot of topics you can talk about already, but just for clarity sake, some more topics include:

- **The Weather**

It's easy. It's neutral. Everyone can talk about it. It's a great starting off point. When you're just starting out on your journey to becoming more confident with your small talk, this is a great topic to practice and to use to improve your skills.

> *I wonder who ordered this beautiful weather?*
>
> *It's like monsoon season today.*
>
> *I love days where the fog is like this. It's so eerie.*

- **Entertainment**

Another firm favorite. People are bound to be interested in something during their free time, whether that's books, movies, TV shows, cinema, sports, restaurants, and basically any form of leisure activity. Jump in and find out what other people like.

> *Any great books you're reading at the moment? I need some good recommendations.*
>
> *Do you listen to podcasts? I'm trying to get into them.*
>
> *Do you have any fun apps on your phone?*

What team do you support?

Been to the movies recently? I haven't been in so long!

Are you watching the tennis championship at the moment?

- ### *Personal Life*

You don't want to get too personal with people you've just met (this can be seen as being too forward or even intrusive), but a few personal questions that help you get to know someone better is fine.

Where does your family come from originally?

Have you ever looked into your heritage?

How long have you and your partner been together?

Do you have brothers and sisters? (Pets is also a decent question)

I'm sure you get the idea. Other great topics you can talk about include:

- *Hobbies*
- *Travel*
- *Food interests*
- *Celebrity gossip*

- *Information on hometown*
- *Work-life and career*

If you're really struggling for ideas, you can always talk about what is happening right here, right now in the location you're in. Listen carefully to find relatable topics that both you and the other person find interesting. If one of you isn't interested in sports at all, then it's not a good place to go unless you're talking about how uneducated you are in sports, which can be quite humorous when communicated in the right way).

Keep asking questions and let the topics of conversation involve naturally.

Small-Talk Topics You MUST Avoid

I've spoken a lot about small-talk topics you can dive into, but very little on topics you should probably avoid talking about at all costs, which is what I'm going to dedicate this section to. It's very easy to get caught out and stuck in talking about these topics, and while they may be okay with some people, generally speaking, I would steer clear of them.

Quick note: That's not to say you can't ever talk about these things with other people in your life, but they're usually reserved for conversations with people you can trust, and you know you respect and can speak openly with.

- **Finances**

I mean, imagine if someone came up to you and asked you how much you earned. You probably wouldn't be very willing to share because it's a personal topic. What's more, how much we earn would only usually be asked as a way to judge someone on who they are, which nobody wants. Avoid at all costs (no pun intended).

- **Religion**

Always a controversial topic. You never know what other people believe, so you're going to want to save this topic until you know someone and have enough respect to listen to each other and actually talk about how you feel on the subject, rather than making snap judgments on someone you barely know.

- **Politics**

Hand in hand with religion, the topic of politics has the potential to get really emotionally charged and out of hand, especially when you're unaware of the views of the other person. There could be a time and a place where it's fine, but generally speaking, avoid this topic until you know someone really well.

- **Death**

This topic should probably be on this list without needing to mention it, but if you're trying to enjoy a positive conversation with someone you want to get to know, you should perhaps avoid such heavy topics like death and loss. These can be emotionally driven and upsetting, not feelings you want to be associated with in your initial meetings.

- **Sex**

Sex is personal. Making jokes, dropping innuendos, and talking openly about sex with strangers has the potential to make people feel really uncomfortable and will remember you in a bad light. Sure, there are times, perhaps if you're flirting, where it could be the perfect time to talk about it, but you're going to want to pick your moments wisely.

- **Health and well-being**

Have you ever been speaking to someone, and you've accidentally dropped that you're not feeling well, and suddenly they jump in with all these quick fixes and remedies? It's the most annoying thing, especially when the other person has no idea about the details of your condition or the complexity of it (nor are they usually a trained healthcare professional). Don't be that person.

• Personal life gossip

By all means, talk about celebrity gossip because these are people who put their lives out there in the public eye, but sharing gossip about people in your life is not a good idea. While people may be engaged and interested in what you're saying, this kind of topic paints you in a negative light, and people will consciously avoid you in case you end up sharing personal information about them.

• Offensive jokes

Sure, you can use your most sexist, racist, and most out-there offensive jokes when you're around people you love, whether that's friends or family. I'm not advocating hate, but I understand that comedy is comedy, no matter what form it takes. However, it's extremely dangerous ground to share these with people you don't know and could end up getting you in a lot of trouble. Imagine sharing one on your first day at work in a new office and pushing everyone away. It's a bad situation to be in.

• Physical appearance

Quite a traditional topic to avoid. It's best not to ask how old someone is or comment on their physical appearance, just because you don't know how sensitive someone may be. A common example of this is asking someone how far in their pregnancy they are when they're not even pregnant. Imagine being in that situation.

- **Ex-partners or friendships**

If you're on a first date with someone, it's pretty common knowledge that you're not going to want to start talking about your exes. It's a bitter place to take the conversation, and it's probably going to make the conversation turn negative, which is not something you want to be connected with when people are spending time with you. Avoid!

- **Any limited conversation topics**

Let's say you start talking about your hobbies— swimming, for example—but the other person has absolutely no interest in swimming and hasn't even swum in years. Why are you going to keep going on about swimming? It's as though you're trying to bore and push away the other person. If someone doesn't seem interested in the topic of conversation, switch it up.

Ending the Conversation

In many ways, how you end your conversations is just as important as how you start them. While you've already created your first impression, how you end an interaction will determine your *lasting* impression and how people treat you the next time you see them. This is why it's a good idea to practice and rehearse some key exit lines you can always fall back on to leave a positive lasting impression. Here are some ideas to get you started.

It has been really great meeting you. Do you have a number or social media?

I can't wait to hear how your project/meeting/event goes. See you next time?

Well, this has been great. I'm going to grab something to eat. See you around?

Wow. It's true you learn something new every day. Thank you for that. I've got to rush off now, but would it be okay to swap details and carry this on another time?

You'll need to adapt what you say, the words you use, and the way you say what you say depending on the situation you're in, just like we've done in every aspect of conversation before. For example, you're going to speak differently to a professional-client than you would someone you're asking on a date, but you can get creative.

The best idea, however, is to have some ideas of how you can positively sign off on a conversation, make your exit, and leave the situation so that the person you were speaking with will remember you and this experience positively.

Practicing the Art of Small Talk

All of these methods and topics we've covered in this chapter are great when it comes to being better at small talk, but as I keep saying, just reading about them now isn't going to make a difference to how good you are. It's only through practice that you'll get better.

I love the metaphor, so I'm going to say it again (probably the last time, though, I promise...maybe).

If you want to get good at swimming, you need to spend time in the pool.

If you're wondering how you're supposed to "get in the pool" when it comes to small talk, this section has got you covered as we explore some of the ways you can integrate small talk into your everyday life, thus becoming better at it.

Keep Your Eyes Open for Opportunities

By speaking with lots of different people about lots of different topics, you'll start to develop your own opening and closing statements, and you'll start to get a real feel for how you can traverse various topics of conversation and what subjects you can talk about passionately. However, these are all social aspects that come with experience, so get the experience!

No matter what you're doing in your life and what situation you're in, keep your eye open for opportunities to practice small talk.

Talk to the cashier at the store. The person behind you in line. The man at the bar. The class teacher after the lesson. I can't stress enough how much practicing is going to benefit you. Of course, not everyone is going to be interested in talking for whatever reason, but that's okay. Just keep going and keep getting better. Step outside your comfort zone!

Pretend You are Friends

When it came to my personal small-talk improvement journey, this was perhaps the biggest game-changer that opened so many doors. I worked in sales for a lot of years and found it difficult talking to new clients and project managers. I could present my projects and proposals because I had direction but was useless when it came to anything outside of that.

However, as soon as I switched my mindset into believing that anyone I was speaking to was already a friend, someone I knew, or someone I could trust and was close to, I unconsciously started treating them as friends, which meant I was more open, more confident, and more charismatic.

It's a quick mental shift—a trick, if you like—that can help alter your perspective into relaxing and being more comfortable in your own skin.

Be Patient with Yourself

Throughout any self-improvement journey, you're going to make mistakes. While these can be embarrassing, especially when it comes to talking with new people you're trying to have a positive relationship with, it's all part of the journey and a part you're going to look back on in years to come and laugh at while reveling in how far you've come.

Messing up is not a big deal, and if you try to protect yourself in life so you never mess up, you're never going to get anywhere or learn the lessons that will change your life.

Set Objectives

While small talk with someone is not a military operation, although it can sometimes feel like it, it can really help you have direction with what you say if you're setting goals and targets for your conversations. Take Kyle at his sister's wedding. Is he trying to have a good time? Get to know people? Have a laugh? Meet someone?

Having a clear objective helps you to determine what kind of energy you're bringing to the table, what kind of topics you want to cover, and what kind of people you're going to invest your time speaking to.

The Summary

And that's it! That wasn't too bad, was it? When it comes to mastering small talk, the core points you're going to want to focus on practicing are:

- Being energetic and enthusiastic
- Be genuinely yourself regarding your interests
- Become confident with a range of small-talk topics
- Practice ending conversations strongly
- Practice small talk when and where you can
- Act like close friends with strangers
- Have conversational goals with people
- Remember that practice makes perfect!

Everything we've spoken about within this chapter should give you a deep enough insight into small talk that you can become a master of it. As I said before, take the points and strategies that resonate with you and apply them to your own life. Don't try and apply everything at once because that's just overwhelming and unsustainable. Take your journey to getting better one step at a time.

Now we can move on to my favorite chapter.

Chapter Seven – Intricate Ways to Be More Charismatic

"Charisma is a sparkle in people that money can't buy. It's an invisible energy with visible effects."

— Marianne Williamson

What does charisma mean to you?

Google defines charisma as being the quality of personal magnetism and charm that you've probably experienced several times in your life. Those are people who speak, and you listen to, and you just can't help but think, *Damn, this person is cool. I want to spend more time with this person and explore what they have to offer.*

I saw this "charm" in the sales industry all the time. I would go into meetings with clients and would listen to companies that would come pitch to us or us to them, and some of the people I saw would have you hanging on their every word from the moment they opened their mouths. They were just so good at public speaking. When they finished, it was like being snapped back into reality, and I was left questioning where I've been the last hour.

Being around a charismatic person is more like an experience than a conversation.

Maybe you've met a boy or girl in a bar and started chatting with them, only to find yourself lost in the experience of them just being, well, them. It doesn't matter how long that experience lasts; you're always left wanting more. They leave an imprint that you don't forget.

If you've watched television shows like *Mad Men, the Queen's Gambit,* and even *Friends,* you'll know that charisma doesn't just come in the standard big ego kind of way. It's not just men in suits who know their industry inside out or women in attractive dresses who act mysterious and subtle that hold people's attention. Very far from it. Perhaps these are traditional views on charisma, but nowadays, these are outdated and barely relevant.

Charisma comes in all different shapes and sizes, and even someone who you may consider a "book nerd," for example, could have so much charisma when it comes to talking about their favorite characters, plot lines, and endings. So, how do you tap into your own pool of charisma? How do you charm others and make them, essentially, attracted to you and the energy you have to offer the world?

Just like small talk and listening, this is a skill that can be learned by understanding a few core truths.

You Own the Situation

What's the one thing that the charismatic people in your life have never been?

Well, they probably have at some points in their lives, but I mean, at the time they were charismatic, what were they not?

I'll give you a clue. It's that same feeling you get when you're about to get on a roller coaster, and you don't know what's going to happen. Is it going to be fun or scary? Are you going to shout or scream? Are you going to pee yourself or throw up? God forbid either hits the kid behind you if you do. Yeah, I'm not a massive fan of theme parks, if you can't tell.

The trait is, of course, nervousness.

Charismatic people have a way of managing their nerves, so they are confident and believe that they are supposed to be a part of the interactions they're in. If you don't feel as though you belong, you're going to feel nervous. If you're putting too much pressure on the outcome of the situation, you're going to feel nervous, and that's just ridiculous when you boil it down to the reality of the situation.

Let's say you're back in college and you see a boy or girl you like, and you want to ask them out.

If you feel nervous, this means you're placing all the importance of the conversation on what their answer is. When someone's answer (the outcome of the situation) becomes the most important part of the conversation, you're not in the moment. Remember how the motivational quotes say life isn't about the destination, but the journey? The same logic applies here.

Doing this means you're creating too much pressure on how the conversation goes. Hence, you're going to believe you need to "act" perfectly in order to get what you want, which is, of course, impossible. Instead, by being present, actively listening, and just having a conversation with this love interest with the goal to enjoy their company right here and now, then it really doesn't matter whether they say yes or no to asking them out, because that doesn't matter. The quality of the interaction you're having is, instead, the most important point.

Paradoxically, when you're not focused on the outcome, there's less pressure, you'll naturally be more charismatic and confident, so if you do ask the other person out, they're having a much more positive time than having to deal with the nervous version of you, and are therefore more likely to say yes.

To summarize, don't put too much pressure on yourself in any social situations. Don't focus on the outcome or the "end goal," but instead focus on enjoying the interaction itself. You'll be less nervous and naturally more charismatic.

Relatability is Key

The subheading says it all. I remember I went to a blood doner's session a few years back, and after you've donated blood, you have to wait ten minutes to make sure you're not going to pass out and everything goes okay. You get a cup of tea and a biscuit, so it's not all bad.

Anyway, one time I was there waiting in the post-donation room, and a guy came and sat next to me. I have no idea how, but we ended up talking, and when I say we, I mean he, about his swimming history, and how to be better at gliding through the water and how to go faster and be more efficient, and then on to all the medals he won, and so on. I'm starting to think swimming is something I should start thinking about introducing to my life with the amount I'm talking about it.

What he was saying was all fine, and some of it was actually quite interesting. Being someone who consciously puts effort into listening, yeah, I may have learned a thing or two, but there was a problem. I couldn't help but not be disinterested in what he had to say because it wasn't relatable at all. I didn't swim, nor did I really care about it. It felt as though he was just using me as an opportunity to talk about himself and his achievements, and I was forced to just go along with everything he said.

That's not a two-way conversation, and it's very boring for me. It would be very boring for anyone.

Apply this in your own interactions and make what you're saying relatable to the person you're speaking with. The more you get to know someone, the easier this will be. However, until you get to that point, try focusing on asking the right questions that will help you understand the other person better, thus being able to choose topics you can both talk about.

Charismatic people include everyone and don't just use conversations to talk about themselves.

Remember People's Names

One of my favorite quotes from Dale Carnegie, one of the most popular and influential authors in sales training and interpersonal skills, is:

"A person's name is the sweetest sound in the world to that person."

And it's true. We all like to be called by our own name, and you should already know how awkward it can be when speaking with someone and you can't remember their name for the life of you. Being like this isn't going to make someone feel special, nor positively relate to you. Taking the time to consciously and purposefully remember someone's name can make a world of difference in your relationships with them. It shows you care and respect that person enough to get to know them properly. These are powerful, charismatic traits. Here are some tips to help:

- Be present when talking to the other person, so you hear their name correctly
- Repeat the person's name back to them to make sure you heard it properly
- Create an association (i.e., Harry with the round glasses)
- Make a rhyme out of their name
- Ask someone else their name if you forgot

Be Funny

I was debating whether I wanted to include this section because yes, if you want to connect with people, being funny and humorous is an extremely good way to go about it, but not everyone is funny in the same way, and we all find different things comical. This may make it hard to connect with others because if your sense of humor is not the same as someone else's, things might not go down too well.

Remember what we said about avoiding offensive jokes? Comedy is hard, especially around strangers.

That being said, a charismatic person will be able to read the room, select the right level of funny, and can make it work. If you have found in the past that you're a naturally funny person, even if you're funny in your own way, then embrace that when the time arises.

Charisma and humor go hand in hand with each other, and being able to put a smile on someone else's face is a priceless gift you should own within yourself. Here are some quick-fire tips to get funnier in your conversations, should you believe you have the potential to be:

- Watch comedy programs and live shows to get ideas of what is funny

- Find and follow comedians you like

- Learn three awesome jokes you like and learn how to tell them perfectly

- Practice not being offended by other forms of comedy

Give, Give, Give

This is another interesting point to think about.

Eric Matthews from Start Co., in an interview with Success.com, said that giving more than you take is one of the most beneficial ways you can be charismatic in the business world, and this also applies to life in general. To be charismatic by nature is to lift up those around you and to make their lives better in some way.

You can do this in simple ways, like giving someone your full attention, or paying them a compliment. You can validate and reassure their thoughts by repeating back what they said.

There's no human on Earth who doesn't want this kind of attention. The real trick here is to first put the other person in the center of your attention. People love this and will be much more willing to converse with you further and deeper.

Second, you can't expect to get anything back. This does, to a degree, suck because a lot of conversations you have can feel very one-sided, but here's a little reminder that you don't always need to speak to that person ever again if they're not someone you want to spend time with and it doesn't become a two-way experience when you're with them. You don't need to be friends with everyone, but that doesn't mean you can't be a charismatic individual.

A few tips for clarity:

- Give genuine compliments if you mean them
- Give someone your full attention
- Don't expect anything in return
- Be polite with good manners

- Be open and honest with the other person (don't wear a mask)

The Summary

Being charismatic is no easy feat, and it takes time and practice. Don't worry if you didn't feel like you got everything you came for in this chapter since this is just an introduction for things you can work on. Give these points some time, and you'll see instant improvements with how charismatic you are. We're going to go deeper in the next chapters.

For reference, the core values you're going to want to remember here are:

- Remember you belong in any situation you're in

- Be relatable to people you're speaking too

- Remember the names of people you speak to

- Let humor come naturally

- Give to people without expecting anything in return

For now, these should be enough little tricks and pointers to keep you going on your way to being a charismatic person who can speak to anyone. Granted, it's not easy stuff, and it's going to take a bit of practice, but it will all come together in time. Just be mindful of what you're doing, and actually step out of your comfort zone to try new things!

This is the only way you'll see the results for yourself!

Chapter Eight – How to Be More Confident

"The most beautiful thing you can wear is confidence." —
Blake Lively

Hand in hand with being charismatic, there's the ability to be confident. Be honest—you saw this coming, and believing you have a lack of confidence is probably one of the reasons you picked up this book in the first place. If so, this is the chapter that's going to help, but I'm hoping you can see how everything we've spoken about already ties into each other and will naturally help you become more confident, simply because you have more strategies to implement within your upcoming conversations.

Being charismatic and being confident are two different things, although they support each other wholeheartedly.

By dictionary definition, being charismatic is having a charm that makes people want to be around you and spend time with you; being confident is having the belief to know that the outcome of a situation will be favorable to you. In other words, you're able to go into a conversation knowing that everything is going to be alright and you're not going to be embarrassed or make a mistake, and even if you do, then you know everything is still going to be okay.

Remember what we were talking about in the last chapter about asking someone on a date? If you feel nervous and unconfident, then you're going to act nervous and unconfident, and the whole situation becomes a bit of a self-fulfilling prophecy. On the other hand, if you're confident and carry yourself well, the chances you'll get a date increase dramatically.

So, how do you do it? Let's find out.

Fake It 'Til You Make It

You've probably heard this saying from time to time, but the science exists that suggests that *acting* a certain way is one of the best ways to *become* a certain way. In other words, if you pretend to be confident, then you will actually become confident.

In psychology and neuroscience, this is known as the Hebbian Principle. How it works is that when a human being does something, which can literally be anything, the tiny neural circuits in their brain light up and start firing to make the "thing" happen. Say you want to lift your right arm up right now. You think about it, and those circuits start firing to make it happen, sending the signals for your body to lift your arm. Now, you can resist doing it if you really want, but how aware of your arm are you right now?

If you're to lift your arm, then the message sent becomes a "link," and the more you allow this link to happen, the easier it becomes. The human brain likes the easy life, and this is why so many of us have habits. We've done the same habit over and over again so often that we do it without thinking, so the brain saves energy and just "does," rather than spending all its time thinking.

Still with me?

Now, we've evolved so far up to this point that you can actually trick this system into developing new habits or, in this case, entirely new states of mind by purely thinking about doing something. Let's keep it related to confidence.

If you were to get up in the morning, go to the mirror, and act like your most confident self, portraying the level of confidence you want yourself to have, and actively act out how you would be (yes, this means talking to yourself out loud), then over time, you would naturally become more confident because you're firing up those circuits saying that you want to be more confident, and then carrying out that command.

You're actively hard-wiring your brain. It's such a clever technique.

This is why motivational speakers will jump up and down and build up their energy before going on stage. Popular speaker Tony Robbins actually has a mini-trampoline he jumps on just moments before heading in front of the crowd. It's to build up his energy and get his blood flowing, so when it comes to show time, he's already in the high-energy state of mind he needs to be in to deliver.

You can do the same!

Basically, define the type of person you want to be and what level of confidence you want to have, practice it in your free time, and then start to implement this level of confidence naturally in your interactions, and you'll notice an incredible difference! Here are some tips that helped me through this process:

- Watch movies and TV shows and see what kind of people you resonate with to define your style of confidence
- Do the same with people in your life
- Practice in front of the mirror for five minutes every single day
- Experiment with different styles of confidence
- Apply your practices to everyday situations you find yourself in

Overcome Thoughts That Hold You Back

Thoughts that stop you from living the life you want to live and hold you back are known as limiting beliefs, and these are crushing your confidence.

Imagine you're going into a job interview, and you're feeling so nervous. You can't help but think you're going to mess everything up, and you keep playing through all the various negative ways the meeting could go. If you're focusing on the bad stuff, then how can you expect to be confident going forward? You're definitely not going to be your best self.

The way to get around this problem is to become aware of what your limiting beliefs are. You can do this long-term through journaling, meditation, counseling, and doing everything we talked about in the first chapter regarding developing your sense of self. However, there is something we can do right now, and it's a fun little exercise I love.

A Quick Little Exercise

Grab a pen and paper and imagine you are going to meet with someone for the first time.

That could be a new client, a stranger in a cafe or on the street, or you're heading into an unfamiliar situation where you need to talk to people, but you don't really know them very well, if at all.

Take a moment to imagine it clearly, and now write down all the negative thoughts that come up. Do you think these people will think you're weird or annoying? Are you conscious of your physical appearance? Are you worried that they won't like you or will talk down to you? Write down anything that comes to mind.

When you read them back, these are your limiting beliefs and things you're going to need to work on when it comes to becoming confident. These are the thoughts that will hold you back and stop you from reaching your full potential. Of course, there's an infinite number of thoughts that could come up here, and it will take time to work through them all, but fortunately, there are tons of articles, books, and websites that can help you address your issues.

For me, I thought people would believe I didn't know what I was talking about, and I wasn't qualified to share my experience because I was still young. However, after some research, I discovered this is a state of mind called Imposter Syndrome, and I was able to take steps to work on letting these limiting thoughts go.

While a little unrelated, I found this limiting beliefs discovery technique very fun when it comes to looking at your finances. Get your pen and paper again and write down your dream wage you'd like to earn in a year. Now add a zero to the end (the right-hand side end) and write down all the reasons why you can't earn that amount. These are your limiting beliefs, and it can be incredibly interesting to see what comes up!

Adopt Confident Body Language

A leading Harvard psychologist, Amy Cuddy, looked into body language and how the way we act physically affects our mindset, state of mind, and overall confidence. In her studies, she took 42 men and women and had them perform what is known as low and high power poses.

These are basically poses that show how confident someone is. In other words, the stereotypical view of a shy person is crouched over and small, hunched, as though trying to hide and not be noticed. On the other hand, a power pose beaming confidence would be something like the Superman pose, with hands on their hips and their head held high.

In the study, the participants were asked to hold certain poses for two minutes, and then saliva samples were taken.

The results were clear. Those people who had adopted high-power poses, similar to the Superman pose, showed lower cortisol levels (the stress hormone) and increased testosterone levels—both of which indicate the person was more relaxed, more confident, less stressed, and more willing to take rests. And this was all just for adopting a different pose.

Hand in hand with faking it until you're making it, you can feel the effects right now. Assuming you're reading this sitting down, straighten your back, and sit back with your hands behind your head, more commonly referred to as the "President's Pose." It looks like the classic office desk pose where you've completed a sale and cross your legs up on the desk because you're so happy with what you've just achieved, although having your legs on the desk is optional.

Have strength in your pose, widen your chest, and do a pose that reminds you of feeling proud. All the stereotypical poses that come to mind will do. Hold the pose for 30 seconds to a minute. How do you feel? How confident and ready to take on the world does it make you feel? This is just how powerful such a simple act can be. Practice these poses when going into tense situations to become far more confident than you would normally be!

Get Hands-On

Hand in hand with the point above, using your hands as your main expressive form of body language can be a great way to feel, look, and become confident. Research by Carol Kinsey Gorman found that listeners will have a much more positive connection with public speakers who gesture with their hands to exaggerate and communicate their points.

The same works the other way around too. If you're playing with your hair, fiddling with your sleeves or your clothes, or keeping your hands still in between your legs while sitting, this can convey the image that you're nervous or anxious. Take control of your hands and channel your inner energy for whatever topic you're talking about!

Implement Eye Contact

Being able to hold and maintain eye contact is pretty much the cornerstone of confidence. If you look away from someone when they're talking to you, look at the ground, or basically anywhere other than you, then it just oozes a lack of confidence. When someone is ashamed of something they've done, they look at the ground because they can't bring themselves to make eye contact. Even dogs do this!

A Texan study held back in 2013 found that people on average make eye contact between 30 and 60% of the time, but if you're looking to make an emotional connection with someone, then you're going to need to up this to about 60–70% of the time. And it's not easy.

If you're consciously thinking about making eye contact with someone for a longer-than-normal period of time, but it's not something you're used to, then chances are, you're going to feel uncomfortable and maybe even as though you're staring. This will make you nervous, and the whole confidence thing starts to fall apart.

However, there are some tips you can follow to make it easy, and also remember, practice makes perfect, so keep trying!

Firstly, you don't need to lock your eyes on both of the eyes of the other person, but instead, focus on one eye. This may sound a little strange, but it works. If you're still feeling uncomfortable, try looking at their eyebrows. Don't look higher than this or lower than their eye level because it will just feel weird, as though you're not paying full attention. Eyebrows are fine. Practice with yourself in the mirror for better results.

When you're coupling this tip with the others we've been speaking about throughout this book, then you should find yourself naturally being able to make eye contact more and more. Just keep practicing, and the results will come.

Slow Down

It's a common trait that people will speak quickly when they are nervous, and this is especially prevalent with people who are new to public speaking. The idea is that someone speaks as fast as possible so they can finish what they're saying quickly, and then no longer have to talk. However, this is a clear sign you're both nervous and anxious, not only showing this to the other person but also validating your fears with yourself.

The simple solution is to slow down. Consciously slow down the speed at which you're talking.

I'm not saying go monotone and drag everything on, but find a nice pace you're comfortable with (which you can find practicing in the mirror!), and then when you're nervous and find yourself speeding up, you can mindfully slow yourself back down. Research shows that around 190 words per minute are the ideal speaking speed for being comfortable and sending across your message effectively.

The Summary

For now, this should be enough confidence content for you to sink your teeth into to have an idea on how to become more confident in your conversations. Remember, if you look good, you'll feel good, so go into every situation from here on out to have the intention to control your self-image and portray yourself as the person you want to be.

Naturally, you'll become this person, and that's who you'll be! I know it sounds simple, but it really is. We overcomplicate things so much and add so much pressure to being the best version of ourselves that we forget it's the power in the little choices we make that shape our reality.

I love the Matt D'avella way of looking at this. Usually, it's taking the smallest steps that will help you make the biggest leaps, so once you're able to knuckle down these small yet powerful tactics, the bigger benefits will fall into place.

For clarity, the key points we covered for you to remember when it comes to being a more confident version of yourself are:

- **Act confident to become confident!**
- **Work on letting go of your limiting beliefs**
- **Take control of your hand gestures**
- **Make eye contact**
- **Slow down your speaking process**
- **Practice!**

Chapter Nine – How to Tell Stories That Land

"Inside each of us is a natural-born storyteller, waiting to be released." — **Robin Moore**

For as long as humans have been living in caves and painting on the walls, we've been storytellers. This is why thousands of new books are published every year and why the pictures drawn onto the walls of the pyramids recount days gone past. Humans love stories, and one of the best ways to connect with someone is to tell them a good one.

The small-talk topics we've already covered are amazing when it comes to breaking the ice, but the crux of the matter is that many people you'll meet in your life are people who want to engage and interact with interesting people. Traditional small talk will only get you so far before people start looking for real substance in what you're saying to them. There will come a time when people want real stories.

But how can you tell someone a story that's going to captivate them and have them hooked off your every word if you're living a pretty generic, typical, mundane life?

Well, to start with, stop believing that your life is any of those things because it's not. It only feels like it to you because you live it day in, day out, and get to see all those mundane aspects, like brushing your teeth and walking into town.

The actual substance of your life is incredibly interesting because you're the only person in the world who has ever done what you've done, made the decisions you've made, and the only human who will experience what you've experienced in all of humanity to come. I'm not going to get any more philosophical than that for now (I just love how mindblowing that whole thought experiment is), but my point is that we all have interesting lives.

You included.

The problem is that not all of us are born storytellers, but again, like all kinds of communication, it's a skill that can be learned and practiced. If you do this, and you're able to tell stories about your life that hook people off your every word and make them want to know more, you literally will be able to talk to anyone about anything, which, of course, is why we're here.

Finding That Killer Plotline

First things first.

You're not going to be able to tell stories if you don't know any. By this, I'm referring to the skill of being able to look into your own daily life and find stories that matter and that can be retold in a captivating way. I know, the first thought that comes to mind is that your life really isn't that interesting, at least not compared to other people's, surely? It is. You just might need to do some digging.

There are, of course, going to be key moments in your life that will naturally be great stories. The day you get married or go on that first date, and everything is new and exciting. Maybe you go away on vacation for your birthday and have an amazing time. Maybe you went to a protest or saw a global event happen. These are easy stories.

Yet, when it comes to pulling out the stories from your everyday life, you may at first need to dig a little deeper.

> *"So, what do you do for work?"*

> *"I'm a manager in a supermarket."*

Stop. Is that the best, most enthralling, and most exciting way you can present that information? It may not seem like it, but it's this kind of information that can be woven into the foundations of a beautiful story. Try again.

> *"So, what do you do for work?"*

"I'm a manager in a supermarket, although sometimes I feel like I'm a detective. Just the other day, I had to follow a shady-looking guy around the store Mission Impossible-*style who looked like he was going to steal several cases of alcohol."*

Damn, now the creative juices are flowing, and the listener is thinking, *Hold up, a guy in the store stealing alcohol? What happened? Did you catch him? Did he attempt to steal anything?* As with all good stories, you've introduced conflict and a plot. Now the listener wants to know more.

See how you've managed to take the really typical and boring question of "What do you do?" that you could hear literally anywhere from a networking meeting to a BBQ with mutual friends, but your response has suddenly drawn in the attention of everyone around you? All it took was a few extras words and a few extra seconds of talking.

Right now, I want you to try it for yourself, right here, out loud. I've just met you and asked you what you do. Don't worry if this is your first time trying this. I'm only here in writing, and no one is here to judge, so get creative.

So, what do you do?

Layer your response with what you do and a little story that happened to you. Something that's happened in the last month. Whatever comes to mind. At this point, we're just practicing and getting those synapses working. The more you practice recalling, the better the stories that will come up. Here are some tips that can help you spot interesting stories in your life.

- Keep a diary or journal and write down everything that's interesting that stands out. You'll be amazed at how much you forget by the end of the day.

- Practice meditation and gratitude; a great way to improve your focus as you go about your day

- Put yourself in interesting situations. Take the long road to work. Speak to new people and see what comes up. You never know what experiences will come your way.

- Make notes on your phone of things that happen and practice dramatizing them.

Writing Your Story Collection

Okay, you don't actually need to write a memoir of short stories about your life, but having a few stories in the bank that you can use when replying to commonly asked questions can be a great idea because they'll be well-rehearsed (at least they will be over time) and you'll have experience in retelling them (even if at first that is just telling them back to yourself in the mirror).

Some topics you can gather up for some of these mini-stories include:

- Your job, career, or occupation
- Something that has happened in the last week
- Any plans you've got coming up in the future
- Stories about your local area
- Stories about the hobbies you do

Last weekend, I watched a pretty mediocre samurai movie, but the ninja guy main character would meditate while working on his bonsai trees. I felt so inspired by the whole scene that I bought myself a bonsai growing kit, the seeds of which I planted this week. I thought you just planted the seeds in the dirt and waited for them to grow, but oh no. The instructions said to soak them in water for 48 hours and then put them in the fridge, where they'll sit for two months. The crazy bit? The seeds turned the water a solid, swamp-water green. So green, in fact, I dropped it out of shock, and it stained my worktops. I'm still trying to scrub it out today.

In reality, I'm just living my life and trying a new little pastime, but this is just a brief example of how you can take an everyday situation of your life and share it in a way that makes people listen. However, this story in itself is not perfect, but I'll show you how and why in the following section.

For now, keep thinking of your own story ideas! Let's try again.

> *"Hey! Welcome back to the grind time. How was your weekend?"*
>
> *"Yeah, not bad. I watched Netflix."*
>
> *"Fun."*
>
> *"Yup."*

Woah. Great story. Not mundane in the slightest. Let's try that again, but this time, let's bring a story element into it.

> *"Hey! Welcome back. How was your weekend?"*
>
> *"My weekend was fine, but it was nothing compared to Friday night. My cat went crazy and started jumping on all the furniture and got stuck on a cabinet. We had to poke her down with a stick."*
>
> *"Wait, what?!"*

As you can see, finding these little stories from your life makes for a much greater conversation. You're replying to the general small-talk questions people use, but you're not giving the boring answers that, let's face it, nobody really wants to hear. People want to talk. Yes.

We're social creatures. But answering small-talk questions can be great up to a point, but in reality, people want more. After all, isn't that what you want from your conversations?

So, how do you find these interesting stories in your life? After all, poking your cat down from a cabinet with a stick is just something you need to do, but to other people, it could be comedy gold. How do you figure out the difference between the mundane and the interesting?

In all honesty, anything can be a good story. It's the way you tell it, which is what is going to attract people. The best way to figure this out is to think about what you find interesting in a story. These are the stories you'll be most passionate about.

Some questions to help you figure this out are:

- Do you like silly stories about pets?
- Do you like exciting, unbelievable, reality-is-stranger-than-fiction type stories?
- Do you like wholesome stories?
- Do you like serious stories?
- Do you like informative stories?
- Do you like stories on current affairs?
- Do you like cute, loving stories?

Whatever kind of story you like, this is the kind of tale you're going to be able to tell with the most energy and passion, so start taking note of what happens. On top of this, you'll need to remember that a good story will always have something relatable in it, which is the element that we'll resonate with the most.

This is why people like gossip, happy endings, and embarrassing moments. We've all been there, and we know what it feels like, for better or for worse, all feelings that make these stories a little more impactful. We all love stories that make us *feel*.

How to Tell a Good Story

There are, of course, infinite ways you can tell a story. You could tell a micro-story, like the ones in the examples we've spoken about above, or you could share a full-on tale. Think sitting around the campfire telling longer tales to one another. Either way, how do you tell a story that people are actually going to want to listen to?

Consider the Length

The length of your story will depend on the context of the situation you're in. If you're chatting with someone in a line, you don't want to go on and on, potentially holding them up and irritating them. If you're an anxious kind of person, then telling a longer story may mean there's more time for you to worry about the delivery of what you're saying. In this case, it would always be better to stick to shorter stories until you're feeling more confident.

Always judge the length of your story based on the situation you're in. You can adapt the length of your story by changing how much detail you give. If you've been engaging in small talk with the listener already and you've already established some common ground, then try to include details that are going to specifically resonate with them.

Choosing the Right Details

Personally, I found that using the 1:1:1 method is the best way to tell people short stories. Each '1' stands for:

- One action
- One sentence summary
- One emotion

For the sake of brevity, a short story should include every one of these in some way. It's not as overwhelming as it may first appear. See if you can spot each element in the following stories.

I went on a date last week and immediately dropped my plate of food onto my lap. I didn't know what to do, so I just got up and left without saying anything—such an embarrassing situation.

I was crossing the road the other day, and a taxi swung around the corner and almost hit me. I was so scared I nearly pooped myself!

We accidentally deleted the client project and had to start from scratch. We worked 16 hours a day for two weeks, but when it was finished, man, there's no better feeling.

As you can see, in just two sentences, there's an action that the story is based around, the story itself is short and sweet, and there's an emotion that makes the story relatable. Now you can expand on these stories as much as you wish, adding in details, jokes, more emotions, and so on, but that's all up to you and your personal style when it comes to storytelling.

The trick to using the 1:1:1 method is to be able to summarize your story in just one sentence and to start close to the end of the clinch of your story. Start close to the "grit" so you give as much information as possible in the least amount of time.

A great way to remember this strategy is to imagine a story about a jailbreak taking place. It doesn't matter if you describe what happens in one sentence or write an entire book on the event. The endpoint of the story is that the jailbreak happened.

Building on Your Stories

Using the 1:1:1 method is perhaps the easiest way out there to tell a good short story that people are going to want to listen to. Those three factors always make a great foundation to build your story on (and works as a standalone) since you can add as much or as little detail as you want or need.

Some people will make do with little details, but some people are going to want to hear more of what you have to say, so how do you keep your conversational momentum flowing? You use structure.

I'm going to list out the points that make up a story structure, but you can add and adjust them however you see fit. This is the same process that the cartoon studio Pixar uses when creating and writing their stories. This is literally the step-by-step guide they use when making their movies, so take note!

- *Setting the foundations*

Setting the stage of the story. Here you introduce characters and build the world. Only use this section if it affects the rest of the story. Otherwise, you can easily skip this part most of the time.

- *Introduction*

Usually, in the first section, you'll introduce a character and their life, what their routine is, and build up tension for the rest of the story. Make this bit quick so you can get to the exciting part.

- **Introduce conflict**

A big event happens, something that disrupts the normal flow of life and throws a spanner in the works. Make sure you include the emotion of what happens here. This is the moment everything flips upside down.

- **The consequences of conflict**

How has the conflict and change affected everything? What are the consequences of the event taking place?

- **Further consequences**

If necessary, add more consequences to really drive home what is going on and how big the event was. You can skip this bit, but usually, two conflicts are ideal.

- **MORE CONSEQUENCES**

You can really drive home your points with even more conflict. (I'll show you in the example below how this works well.) The more emotional resonance you have in the last three stages, the more emotionally attached to your story your listener will be!

- **Conclusion**

What does the main character do in the story to deal with or resolve the conflict? What action needs to be taken? What problem needs to be solved, and how *does this happen? Conclude how the story is wrapped up.*

- ● **Aftermath**

What happened after the conflict was resolved and everyone has moved on? More emotion here. Is it a better or worse ending? How have the characters been affected by the event?

Of course, this is a lot to take in, but don't let it overwhelm you. If something happens to you in your life that you want to remember, and you think it's going to make a great story, take some time to remember the details.

Later, you can then adjust your story and build on it, so it fits this structure. If you want to keep things simple, you can just remember the general structure of what happened and tell it in order.

I know all of this might seem like a lot, to begin with, and you may even be thinking that surely this is not how people tell great stories? It's so much behind-the-scenes work, but then when you think about the performances of motivational speakers and stand-up comedies, this is exactly the level of effort they put into their stories, which is what makes them so successful.

Sure, you might not want to go all the way with the structuring and so on, but at least you have this knowledge to work with, and you know how it all works. Let's say something happens, and you know this is a good story to tell other people. You might want to work on how you're adding emotions into your tale, or highlighting the conflict of what happened, and so on. With practice and experience, your stories will just get better and better.

Ultimately, this is all with the aim of allowing you to share your stories more naturally while still understanding where to apply details in the right places.

Here's an example story to show you exactly how this structure works.

I was heading to work driving along the main road; you know the ones with the trees and fields along the side? I was behind this lorry, and there was a car up front with hazard lights on, parked at the side of the road. I slowed down, and suddenly this dog ran out into the road.

The truck swerved to miss it, which it did by such a tiny amount, and it jumped the ditch and ran into the woods. The truck carried on, and I pulled over to the side. The woman in the front of the car was crying her eyes out, having a panic attack as her dog had jumped out the window while she was driving, and she couldn't get it to come back. It kept coming back, running across the road, and then back again, thinking it was a game.

I stayed with her for half an hour while another car pulled over, and the man inside helped. We walked through the woods and eventually managed to get hold of the dog and bring it back to the owner, who started crying in happiness. It was such a heartfelt moment. She vowed never to drive with her windows all the way down again.

True story, by the way.

This is a casual story written in the way you would say it out loud, maybe in response to "Why are you late for work?" and while it contains all the elements you'd look for in a story, it's a little long and can be refined to become more comprehensive. Here's an edited version with the structure highlighted.

*(**Introduction**) I was driving down a country road and saw a car parked up ahead, the hazard lights blinking. (**Conflict**) As I slowed down to see if I could help, a dog suddenly ran out into the road, right in front of an oncoming truck (**Consequence**). Thank God it missed it, but it was only by just enough.*

*The truck swerved, and the dog jumped the ditch and ran back into the woods. (**Consequence**) I pulled over and saw the woman in the parked car. Through tears, she told me she was having a panic attack (**consequence**) since her dog jumped out the window*

135

while she was driving, and she couldn't get it to come back. It kept running across the road and then back into the woods, thinking it was a game.

*I stayed for half an hour while another driver and I came to help. We walked through the woods and finally managed to get hold of the dog and bring it back to the owner. (**Resolution/Conclusion**) It was so beautiful seeing her face light up. She vowed never to drive with her windows all the way down again. (**Aftermath**)*

Now, you're probably not going to have enough time to think and edit your story as you say it when you're in a real-life conversation, which is why I say you should take some time to get familiar with this structure in your own time. You don't need to do this for every story that matters, just the ones that count.

The point is to get to grips with these skills and this structure of storytelling that all comes with practice and awareness that this is how it all works. I've lost count of how many hours I've spent in front of the mirror or tidying up my house, just talking to myself and experimenting with the best way to tell a story like this to someone.

However, the benefits of this practice and this behind-the-scenes work have always paid off when I'm around the water cooler, and everyone is hooked on my every word.

The Summary

In your life, be mindful of events and situations you find yourself in and be aware of them. They can be the most mundane of experiences, but how you tell the story (and how much energy you put into it) is everything and is what will make you a great, charismatic, and confident storyteller.

Whenever you find a story in your life you want to hold on to, set to work on organizing the structure, identify the various elements that make the story great, and you'll be able to bring them all together to tell a story about your everyday life that will captivate and wow anybody you're speaking to.

And so, bringing all this together, you should now have the ability to come up with compelling stories of events that happen in your life, not only picking good story ideas but also telling your stories in creative, captivating ways that will blow your listeners away.

Chapter Ten - Becoming an Interesting Person

*"Your life is your canvas, and you are the masterpiece. There are a million ways to be kind, amazing, fabulous, creative, bold, and interesting." — **Kerli***

When my social anxiety was at its peak, I was roughly 22 years old, and it seemed as though my life consisted of nothing more than going to work, going home, playing video games, and that's about it. I wasn't going out and doing anything, I wasn't having new experiences, and I certainly wasn't making memories that were going to last a lifetime.

While in the last chapter we spoke about the fact you can make stories sound interesting, regardless of what is actually happening in your life, there's no doubt that you can be proactive in making your life more interesting by changing a few simple things. The thing is, not only will doing more with your life make you more interesting to talk to since you'll have more to talk about, but you're also going to be happier with yourself and your life. Thus, you're going to be more confident, more charismatic, and more yourself.

Come on, be honest. Raise your hand if you've found yourself stuck in some bad habits that don't bring value into your life? Maybe you binge entertainment, haven't created anything for a long time, or you have dreams of doing something, starting something, or going somewhere, but you're always putting it off, even though you don't really have a reason why.

This was my relationship with writing for many years.

For as long as I can remember, I wanted to write books. I loved the idea of writing, and throughout my early twenties, I would write here and there, but I never put effort into making it a proper habit. I would go weeks and then months without writing anything, and it never really progressed anywhere. I can't tell people I'm writing or want to be a writer if I'm not writing, so something had to change.

I want to dedicate this chapter to sharing some tips and advice that I found helpful when it came to becoming a more interesting person and ultimately lead a more fulfilling life. In the very real sense, this isn't for anybody else but yourself, but there's no doubt that doing more interesting things, or at least becoming aware and educated about more things in life, will help you connect more effortlessly with other people.

As a quick note, notice how I'm not saying you need to do *more* with your life. This chapter is more focused on helping you realize what's important to you, what fuels your sense of self (see chapter one), and then giving you the intention to cut out everything else that doesn't actually serve you nor brings value to your existence.

Okay, I'm sure you get the point. Let's jump into the tips.

Read More Books

A really simple tip to get us started. How many books do you have at home that you've been excited to read but just haven't got around to doing it yet, nor do you really have any solid plans to start? That's me all over. My hobby is just buying new books that I never actually read.

Reading is such an amazing pastime because it can not only be entertaining and an absolute joy to read and get lost in other worlds and the lives of fictional characters, but it opens the doorway to more opportunities than you can ever imagine.

For example, I just finished reading *Dark Matter* by Blake Crouch (which I highly recommend), which talks about Multiverse theory and quantum mechanics.

The story is incredible and one of my favorite books in a long time (I read the whole thing in one sitting), but I also was interested in learning more about quantum mechanics. Now, I definitely don't understand how it all works, but I went down the rabbit hole and ended up discussing it all with someone at work who shared a love for the same thing.

This opportunity came from reading. If I didn't read the books, I wouldn't be connecting with my colleague in a new, interesting, and meaningful way. You never know what opportunities are right around the corner. Some tips to help you read include:

- Find some books you love. Fiction or non-fiction. Get a stack of them and make your way through the list.

- Try books you would never normally try, just to see what they're like.

- Find books you're interested in that inspire you, educate you, and make you want to try and explore new things in life.

If you need any further convincing to start a reading habit, there's endless research that found that the activity of reading trains your brain to be better at processing information. It can also reduce your risk of age-related cognitive decline, lowers your risk of conditions like dementia (proven with a large 14-year study and another 2018 study in China carried out on 16,000 people), reduces stress, and helps you live longer.

Switch Up Your Routine

One of the best and most simple changes I have made over the last two years is occasionally setting my alarm much earlier than normal, so I get up at silly o'clock in the morning (usually around 5 a.m.) and then walk to the highest point in my city and watch the sunrise. It's a strange little ritual I do perhaps once a month, and it really does bring so much joy into my life.

Switching up your routine and doing things "just because" is a great way to keep you on your toes and keep things in your life interesting. When it comes to conversations, I can share my experiences (I sometimes even take the people I'm talking to next time I go, and we enjoy it together). It makes for interesting experiences that break up the monotony of everyday life that we all fall victim to every now and then.

What's more, you never know what other experiences you're going to have when you go on an unplanned whim. The last time I did the hike, I saw a group of baby foxes rummaging through bins, and it was such a beautiful sight. I would have missed it all had I stayed in bed.

Volunteer Your Time

Volunteering your time is a win-win for everyone involved.

Not only are you dedicating some time of your life to help others and actually benefit the communities or causes you're working for, but you also become more interesting because of the experiences you're getting involved in.

My partner and I spent a few months in 2020 helping out at a cat shelter. It wasn't the best experience since I spent most of the time cleaning out cages and washing some of the cats, but it was so interesting to see how the cats come in, what the process is for dealing and rehoming cats, and just seeing how difficult and tough it can be for both the humans and animals.

It's all a learning experience, and it can all bring so much into your life if you're willing to let it in.

Embrace Fear

An actionable tip you can try right now. Whenever you go to do something new, or you're entering an experience that you aren't sure about, do you get that little pang in your stomach? That fear that you don't really know how to move forward? Notice that feeling and try to step through it. Embrace the fear, and don't let it hold you back.

Will Smith famously said in an interview that "Everything that's good in life can be found on the other side of fear." You just need to take the leap of faith in yourself. Remember, the fear of being uninteresting makes you uninteresting. These emotions shut you down and hold you in place, rather than allowing you to live free.

Invest Your Time Wisely

It's common knowledge that the only real resource you ever have to invest in your life is the time you're alive. Even when you're working, you're basically exchanging your time for money. While there are things that we have to do to survive, it can change so much when you really start to see where your time is going.

Are you watching TV all the time? Binging your social media feeds? Going to the same vacation spots every year? Drinking and partying every weekend? Sure, if you're doing what you love, then keep spending your time in that way. That's fine.

However, this is definitely not the case for all of us, and so many of us face the very real realizations that we're probably wasting our lives. If you want to be interesting and feel as though you can get more out of life, start treating your time as a currency, and look at where you're spending it.

Have Interesting Conversations

If you're asking someone how they are, but you don't really care about the answer, this is going to show up like a house on fire.

Lazy, uninteresting people stick to small-talk topics like the weather and ask if they're watching any good TV series (remember that watching most TV is just a passive activity that won't really bring you any gain), or ask what you do for a career. BORING! It's fine every now and then, and when you're starting out, but after everything you've read so far, you're definitely beyond this point now.

Instead of boring topics, open the doorway to new, interesting conversations, like asking what personal projects someone is working on, what the weirdest thing they have ever eaten is, what items you could find on their bucket list, or if they're learning any new skills.

Getting answers to these questions can introduce you to whole new worlds that you didn't even know existed. You never know—you might be introduced to something new that you love, or you may learn something new that changes your life.

Try New Hobbies

This doesn't really need a lot of explaining, so I'll be brief.

At the beginning of 2020, I sat down and wrote down all the things I actually care about. I enjoyed writing. I liked to explore spiritual concepts, like meditating and lucid dreaming. I wanted to learn to speak French. I wanted to learn how to play chess properly. I wanted to read more books. I wanted to learn how to play the Blues guitar. This was simply me sitting down to write a list of all the hobbies I wanted to get involved in.

Take a pen and paper right now and write down all the things you're interested in and would love to get involved in. Even if you've never really given the activity or hobby much thought before, but it's more of a fleeting idea, still write it down.

These are all the things you care about, and you know you did because you took the time to write them down! Now figure out which hobbies you love the most and which ones you want to get involved in. Make time for them and enjoy the experience you have doing them! Not only will you meet new people, but you'll also have interesting things to talk about with others!

The Summary

There are endless ways you can be proactive and become a more interesting person, thus having more to talk about and just being more satisfied with the way you're spending your life. Everybody has what it takes to be more interesting. It's just a matter of taking action into your own hands.

Sure, you might just need to work on breaking out of some old habits, replacing them with good ones, and overcoming the fear that's holding you back, but this is where you need to exercise patience and believe in the long term. Remember, little steps help you make giant leaps.

Chapter Eleven – Developing Meaningful Relationships

*"Each friend represents a world in us, a world possibly not born until they arrive, and it is only by this meeting that a new world is born." — **Anais Nin***

And here we are. We've arrived at the final part of this book. As you can see, the final title of this book reads "Developing Meaningful Relationships," but so far, we've spent all our time on conversations and being able to talk to anyone about anything, which you should be able to do by now. However, the last question that remains is simple.

How can you go from knowing someone and wowing them with your charm, confidence, and small talk, and then actually develop a proper relationship with them? How can you meet people and become true friends with them?

It's a weird thought that so many of us are becoming more and more disconnected in a world that's more hyper-connected than ever before. I can't remember entirely, but when I was a kid back in school, it seemed like making friends was so easy. Sure, you wouldn't get along or like the company of everyone (it would be weird if you did), but there were no inhibitions in talking to new people. You would just chat about whatever was going on, and if you got along, you became friends.

It feels like there's an underlying level of pressure and anxiety that stops things today from being that easy. It's a cringey thought to imagine walking up to someone and just talking to them and then becoming lifelong friends. Maybe in an ideal world, right? Maybe you believe that logic only works in the movies? It's not. It just takes some time and effort to see what life can alternatively be like.

Taking everything you know so far, how can you go from meeting someone for the first time, small talking with them, telling them stories, charming them with your charisma and confidence, and then ultimately becoming friends with them, or at least developing a meaningful relationship of some kind?

This chapter is all about showing you how.

The Benefits are Unparalleled

While having strong connections with people in your life and talking to lots of people is definitely going to make you feel less lonely and more charismatic and confident, having a million acquaintances is no substitute for having five friends that you have a deep and meaningful connection with.

Research shows that having proper connections with people can bring so many benefits into your life; it's hard to know where to begin. A 2014 study carried out by the Society for Personality, and Social Psychology, found that meaningful relationships will:

- Help you live longer
- Improves many aspects of your mental health
- Improves your ability to judge your own well-being
- Increases your self-confidence
- Provides you with wide perspectives
- Provides you with increased resilience in most aspects of your life

There are even sources that claim that having meaningful relationships is "the healthiest thing you can do for yourself" (Medical Daily, 2014). In other words, focus on developing meaningful relationships. This will bring so much goodness into your life.

Understanding the Barriers

To fully understand how to make close friends, you need to know the things that are holding you back. The two main culprits of this are:

- Technology ruining our attention span, make it harder to concentrate, and emulates the feeling of being connected to those we love and care about

- Having busy lives, such as working full-time jobs, working on side projects, and trying to keep up with the fast-paced life that feels common, as promoted by the "mainstream" way of living.

In other words, just because you see your best friend's name on your Facebook feed, that doesn't mean you're actually connecting with them. You need to put your phone down and reach out to them properly and make time to have actual experiences with them, but more on that in a bit.

Now we're going to explore how to take these initial relationships in your life and move forward, forming stronger bonds than ever before and being able to connect with these people that you might one day say you love.

You Can't Be Friends with Everyone

Before we really get into the tips, make sure you're aware of the fact that you're not going to be friends with everyone, and nor should you try to be.

I'm not saying you should outwardly be blunt and forceful to people you don't like. Stay civil. Instead, if you really feel a natural draw to someone, and you feel a connection is there, then it's definitely something you should pursue. If not, that doesn't matter. You're just a step closer to finding the people who are right in your life.

Spend Time with Your New Friends

As I write this book, the world has been gripped by the COVID-19 pandemic, and it's mixed up the world in ways that we could have never predicted. This has made many of us become more disconnected due to lockdown rules, but the happiest people were the ones who still found a way to connect and spend time together.

If you want to connect with someone and deepen your relationship with them, you need to spend time with them, create memories together, and be in each other's presence, not just online. It's clear that times like the COVID-19 pandemic means that connecting in such an intimate way isn't always possible, but that doesn't mean dedicating time to each other is any less essential.

Whether you're going for a socially distanced walk, hosting online activities like Zoom quiz nights or group Netflix streams, or even just chatting via a video call, spending time with people is a must. Dedicating time to each other (and making sure it's fair both ways) is how relationships grow.

Support Each Other

The latest research shows that friends become closer than ever when they help each other through hard times. This doesn't just mean dealing with a tragedy or trauma, but instead could just be offering support on a friend's self-improvement journey. It's always easier and more effective to go through change with someone by your side.

In a 2008 study, researchers placed some participants at the top of a hill either alone, alongside a stranger, or standing next to a friend. When asked to grade how steep the hill was, the participants who were next to a friend thought the hill to be far less steep than those who were standing alone. In other words, when you're standing with someone you're connected to, the hard times aren't so bad.

Be Yourself

Finally, and perhaps most importantly, be yourself around those you love.

It can be hard sometimes to even acknowledge we're wearing masks around those we love, let alone trying to take them off, but it's never been more important to embrace who you are and just be you.

If you're pretending to be someone you're not with your friends, then eventually, it's going to backfire.

Either you won't be happy or your friends won't, so save yourself the drama and just be unapologetically you. Even if you change over time (which everyone does), real friends will be accepting of exactly who you are.

And that's it! If you can follow these simple tricks and tips, you'll be able to take the people you know and like in your life and turn them into friends that you share a deep, meaningful connection with, and the world becomes your oyster.

The Summary

Relationships are important. If you take everything you've learned in this book but just jump around from person to person, attracting them with your charm, hooking them with your stories and become such a memorable person in their lives, but then move on without creating deeper relationships with people along the way, you're going to feel lonely and unsatisfied with your life.

Take time to invest yourself into your relationships. Sure, you can pick and choose who you're friends with, but it's important to give people a shot. Having lived with social anxiety for many years, I know it can be hard and scary to open up to other people, but trust me when I say it will be one of the best things you ever do.

To recap, some of the elements you'll want to focus on include:

- Understanding what holds you back
- Remember, you can't be friends with everyone
- Spend time with one another
- Always be yourself!

Now it's time to say farewell!

Final Thoughts

And so, we come to the end of our journey, and it's all over to you!

I hope you've enjoyed reading this more than anything, and you've learned a lot. I know I said I was going to say it one last time chapters ago, but here's another for good measure: Don't give up on your learning path! The path to better communication, like all self-improvement journeys, is a continuous learning curve with an infinite skill cap. You can always just keep getting better and better.

However, the only way you're going to do this is by practicing over and over again, being willing to embrace any fears or anxieties you may have in order to overcome them. Just keep at it, take everything we've spoken about with baby steps, and you'll see big improvements in no time at all!

I would love to hear some feedback from you! Whenever you bought the book, hit me up with a review and a few words letting me know what you thought about the book, what you liked, and what you think I could do better.

I'm only a human being doing what I love, but I'm always striving to be better and to give you the best experience I can! I also love hearing all the amazing ways these books help you see life in a different way, so let me know and inspire me to keep going!

Enjoy your journey, and I wish you the best of luck! See you next time!

James

Also by James W. Williams

How to Read People Like a Book: A Guide to Speed-Reading People, Understand Body Language and Emotions, Decode Intentions, and Connect Effortlessly

Communication Skills Training: How to Talk to Anyone, Connect Effortlessly, Develop Charisma, and Become a People Person

How to Make People Laugh: Develop Confidence and Charisma, Master Improv Comedy, and Be More Witty with Anyone, Anytime, Anywhere

Digital Minimalism in Everyday Life: Overcome Technology Addiction, Declutter Your Mind, and Reclaim Your Freedom

Self-discipline Mastery: Develop Navy Seal Mental Toughness, Unbreakable Grit, Spartan Mindset, Build Good Habits, and Increase Your Productivity

How to Make People Like You: 19 Science-Based Methods to Increase Your Charisma, Spark Attraction, Win Friends, and Connect Effortlessly

How to Make People Do What You Want: Methods of Subtle Psychology to Read People, Persuade, and Influence Human Behavior

References

Active Listening Skills, Examples and Exercises. Virtualspeech.com. (2021). Retrieved 2 March 2021, from https://virtualspeech.com/blog/active-listening-skills-examples-and-exercises.

Study.com. (2021). Retrieved 2 March 2021, from https://study.com/academy/lesson/sense-of-self-in-psychology-definition-development-quiz.html.

Bhasin, H. (2021). *Types of Listening: What it is, and 18 Different Type of Listening*. Marketing91. Retrieved 2 March 2021, from https://www.marketing91.com/types-of-listening/.

How to Build a Strong Sense of Self. Psychology Today. (2021). Retrieved 2 March 2021, from https://www.psychologytoday.com/us/blog/your-emotional-meter/201908/how-build-strong-sense-self.

Practice Listen to Understand vs. Listen to Respond | CoDevelop. Codevelop.co. (2021). Retrieved 2 March 2021, from https://www.codevelop.co/practice-listen-to-understand-vs-listen-to-respond/?cn-reloaded=1.

Sense of Self: What It Is and How to Build It. Healthline. (2021). Retrieved 2 February 2021, from https://www.healthline.com/health/sense-of-self#importance .

The importance of listening skills. MSU Extension. (2021). Retrieved 2 March 2021, from https://www.canr.msu.edu/news/the_importance_of _listening_skills.

Listening to People. Harvard Business Review. (2021). Retrieved 2 March 2021, from https://hbr.org/1957/09/listening-to-people.

Frost, A. (2021). *The Ultimate Guide to Small Talk: Conversation Starters, Powerful Questions, & More*. Blog.hubspot.com. Retrieved 2 March 2021, from https://blog.hubspot.com/sales/small-talk-guide.

Attention Alert! Study on Distraction Reveals Some Surprises. Psychology Today. (2021). Retrieved 2 March 2021, from https://www.psychologytoday.com/us/blog/rewired-the-psychology-technology/201204/attention-alert-study-distraction-reveals-some.

Kandasamy, N., Garfinkel, S., Page, L. *et al.* Interoceptive Ability Predicts Survival on a London Trading Floor. *Sci Rep* **6,** 32986 (2016). https://doi.org/10.1038/srep32986

Elicitation Techniques | Federal Bureau of Investigation. Federal Bureau of Investigation. (2021). Retrieved 2 March 2021, from https://www.fbi.gov/file-repository/elicitation-brochure.pdf/view.

Krigolson.com. (2021). Retrieved 2 March 2021, from http://krigolson.com/uploads/4/3/8/4/43848243/mcclelland_hebbian_learning.pdf.

Shellenbarger, S. (2021). *Just Look Me in the Eye Already*. WSJ. Retrieved 2 March 2021, from https://www.wsj.com/articles/SB1000142412788732 48098045785112908222228174.

Studio, A. (2021). *The Story Spine: Pixar's 4th Rule of Storytelling*. Aerogramme Writers' Studio. Retrieved 2 March 2021, from https://www.aerogrammestudio.com/2013/03/22/the-story-spine-pixars-4th-rule-of-storytelling/.

Berns, G. S., Blaine, K., Prietula, M. J., & Pye, B. E. (2013). Short- and long-term effects of a novel on connectivity in the brain. *Brain connectivity, 3*(6), 590–600. https://doi.org/10.1089/brain.2013.0166

Chang, Y., Wu, I., & Hsiung, C. (2021). Reading activity prevents long-term decline in cognitive function in older people: Evidence from a 14-year longitudinal study. *International Psychogeriatrics, 33*(1), 63-74. doi:10.1017/S1041610220000812

Lee ATC, Richards M, Chan WC, Chiu HFK, Lee RSY, Lam LCW. Association of Daily Intellectual Activities With Lower Risk of Incident Dementia Among Older Chinese Adults. *JAMA Psychiatry*. 2018;75(7):697–703. doi:10.1001/jamapsychiatry.2018.0657

Meaningful relationships can help you thrive. ScienceDaily. (2021). Retrieved 2 March 2021, from https://www.sciencedaily.com/releases/2014/08/140 829084247.htm.

Iyer, S. (2014, August 29). *Developing Meaningful Relationships Is Probably The Healthiest Thing You'll Do In Life.* Medical Daily. https://www.medicaldaily.com/developing-meaningful-relationships-probably-healthiest-thing-youll-do-life-300464

Schnall, S., Harber, K. D., Stefanucci, J. K., & Proffitt, D. R. (2008). Social support and the perception of geographical slant. *Journal of Experimental Social Psychology, 44,* 1246-1255.

The Psychology of Social Media. (2020, May 5). King University Online. https://online.king.edu/news/psychology-of-social-media/

Primack, B. A., Shensa, A., Sidani, J. E., Whaite, E. O., Lin, L. Y., Rosen, D., Colditz, J. B., Radovic, A., & Miller, E. (2017). Social Media Use and Perceived Social Isolation Among Young Adults in the U.S. *American journal of preventive medicine, 53*(1), 1–8. https://doi.org/10.1016/j.amepre.2017.01.010